Vincent van Gogh

LETTERS FROM PROVENCE

· CONTENTS ·

1 Pear tree in bloom
April 1888.

Foreword

VINCENT VAN GOGH's greatest paintings were done during his three years in Provence. It was here, under the strong light of the Midi, that he captured his sunflowers, orchards, olive groves and harvest scenes. But in addition to his paintings, Vincent left us his letters, a collection of correspondence that enhances our understanding of his pictures. In them Vincent describes the landscape of Provence: the town of Arles, the farmland of the Crau and the mountains of the Alpilles. He writes about his friends and family, most of them far away in Paris or Holland. He discusses his favourite artists and authors, and what they mean to him. He recounts the day-to-day struggle of living without a job—he was dependent on money sent by his brother Theo—and of being ignored by the art world. Most important of all, Vincent writes about his own paintings, often including a little sketch in his letters to explain what he is working on. These sketches, done very quickly and with great spontaneity, capture what he considers are the essential elements of a picture. Vincent's handwriting is also revealing: he has a great variety of styles, even within one letter, which reflect the mood of what he is trying to say.

The majority of Vincent's letters were written to his younger brother Theo, who was an art dealer in Paris. Theo kept Vincent's letters in a drawer in his desk at home in Montmartre and, after his marriage, his wife Jo recalled that 'week after week I saw the soon familiar yellow envelopes with the characteristic handwriting increase in number.' Theo died just six months after Vincent's suicide, aged only thirty-three. His wife treasured Vincent's letters,

recording that on her return to Paris after Theo's funeral the correspondence comforted her: 'The first lonely evening which I spent in our home after my return I took the package of letters. . . Evening after evening that was my consolation after the miserable days. . . I not only read the letters with my heart, but with my whole soul. And so it has remained all the time. I have read them, and re-read them, until I saw the figure of Vincent clearly before me.'

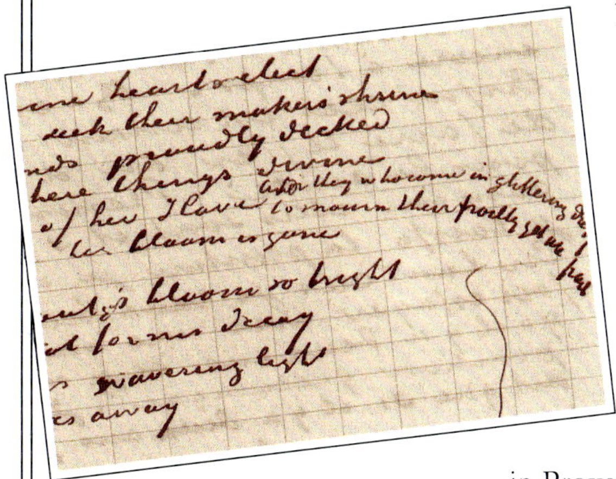
heart elect
seek their maker's shrine
proudly decked
things divine
her I love
bloom is gone
bloom so bright
forms decay
wavering light
away

2 Letter to Wil
Part of an unidentified poem in English, included in Vincent's letter to his sister of 23 December 1889.

Vincent's letters to Theo are not the only ones that survive. The correspondence with his mother and his youngest sister Wil exists as do letters to his artist friends Paul Gauguin, Emile Bernard, Paul Signac, Georges-Albert Aurier, John Russell, Eugène Boch and Arnold Koning, as well as those to the Ginoux family, who were his closest friends in Arles. Considering that it was not until years after his death that Vincent's fame began to spread, it is surprising that so many of his letters have survived. From the three years that Vincent spent in Provence 260 letters survive, extracts from about half of which are included in this book. In making the selection we have concentrated on material that gives an insight into his everyday life and his paintings. One particular letter should be mentioned, since it is published here for the first time in English. This is an important letter to Gauguin that Vincent wrote on 22 January 1889, just a month after the crisis that led him to mutilate his ear.

In addition to focusing on Vincent's stay in the south of France, *Letters from Provence* includes a 'postscript' on the seventy days that he spent at Auvers-sur-Oise, near Paris. It was here that Vincent committed suicide: he climbed up to the wheatfields where he had been painting and shot himself, dying two days later on 29 July 1890. On his body was found a final letter to Theo.

Although Vincent often found it difficult to communicate with people face-to-face, when he took up his pen the ideas flowed. His letters are peppered with references to the writers and artists who inspired him, and show that he was remarkably well-read. Vincent was also a good linguist: most of his letters from Provence were written in French. He also wrote in English, a legacy of his time as a young art dealer in London.

I have referred to Van Gogh as Vincent throughout the text because everyone knew him as Vincent and this was how he signed his paintings.

I would like to thank all those who have helped with this book. The staff of the Van Gogh Museum in Amsterdam gave every assistance at a time when they were busy mounting the centenary exhibition. The guide to further reading at the end of the book acknowledges the published sources that proved particularly useful, but the studies of Dr Jan Hulsker and Professor Ronald Pickvance deserve to be singled out for special mention. Little, Brown and Company and Thames and Hudson Ltd kindly granted permission to use extracts from the published Van Gogh letters; the small numbers at the foot of each letter refer to their edition. (The numbers in square brackets within the text of the letters refer to the illustration numbers.) Kitty Black translated the letter to Gauguin of 22 January 1889. Thanks are due to all those who supplied illustrations, particularly the Van Gogh Museum and the Kröller-Müller Museum in Otterlo. I would also like to thank Gabrielle Townsend of Collins & Brown.

Finally, I hope that the letters will present Vincent's paintings in a fresh light, adding another layer of meaning to them.

Martin Bailey

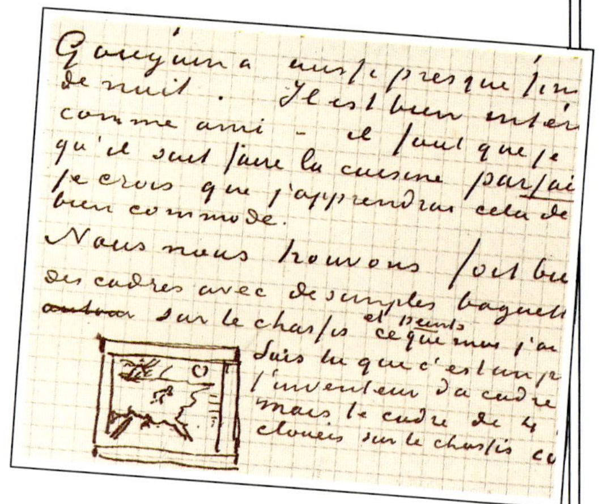
Gauguin a aussi presque fin
de nuit. Il est bien intér
comme ami - il faut que je
qu'il sait faire la cuisine parfai
je crois que j'apprendrai cela de
bien commode.
Nous nous trouvons fort bien
des cadres avec de simples baguettes
sur le chassis et peints ce que moi j'ai
l'inventeur du cadre
mais le cadre de 4
clouées sur le chassis ce

3 Letter to Theo
In this letter of c.*12 November 1888 Vincent explains that Gauguin, who had just arrived in Arles, had suggested an ingenious way of making white picture frames. A tiny sketch was added, showing how Vincent had just framed his painting of 'The Red Vineyard'.*

Introduction

4 SELF-PORTRAIT WITH DARK FELT HAT
One of his earliest self-portraits, painted in Paris in the spring of 1886.

WHEN VINCENT VAN GOGH arrived in Arles, on 20 February 1888, he was almost thirty-five. Although this was to prove his greatest year, in terms of the masterpieces that he produced, he had only started to paint six years earlier. In that short time, he had taught himself. To begin with he had worked in dark colours, depicting the peasants of Brabant. Then, during his time in Paris, he lightened his palette, influenced by the colours of the Impressionists. As he set off for Arles, he was just in the process of developing his highly personal style.

Vincent was born on 30 March 1853 at Zundert, a village in the south of the Netherlands. His childhood seems to have been unremarkable, although he was a rather lonely and awkward boy. His father Theodorus was a Reformed Church pastor and his mother Anna Carbentus ran the family home. The family's eldest son, Vincent had three sisters and two brothers.

Looking back at his career, it is strange to recall that Vincent worked as an art dealer for seven years. This choice of career, made when he left school at sixteen, was probably not an early sign of artistic ability or interest but the result of family connections. Three of his uncles were in the art business and it was Uncle Cent who found a place for his young nephew at Goupil's gallery in The Hague.

In 1873, just after turning twenty, Vincent was transferred to London, where he worked at Goupil's branch in Covent Garden. He found lodgings in Brixton, at 87 Hackford Road, and it was

there that he fell in love with his landlady's daughter, Eugenie Loyer. She rejected his advances, which pushed him into a deep depression; his work suffered badly and his parents, blaming the 'London fog', thought that a change of scene might be the answer. Twice he was temporarily transferred to Goupil's gallery in Paris, but despite his family's links with Goupil's, the gallery became increasingly dissatisfied with their awkward assistant. Early in the New Year of 1876 he was sacked.

By this time Vincent had become increasingly obsessed by evangelical Christianity. This was, it soon became clear, a reaction to the two great rejections he had suffered—the rebuff by Eugenie and the loss of his job at the gallery. Vincent's worried parents encouraged their son to seek another job in the art world, possibly with a museum in London. But he was more interested in a position with the church and thought about becoming an evangelist in an English coalmining town or even a missionary in Latin America. In the end he decided to become a teacher.

On his last day at Goupil's, just before Easter 1876, Vincent received a reply to an application for a job as a teaching assistant in Ramsgate. Although unpaid, he accepted the post in return for board and lodging. The following month the school moved to Isleworth, a village west of London. There Vincent took up preaching, giving his first sermon at Richmond Methodist church on 5 November 1876. 'When I was standing in the pulpit, I felt like somebody who, emerging from a dark cave underground, comes back to the friendly daylight,' he wrote to his brother Theo, who had then taken over his job with Goupil's in The Hague.

At Christmas 1876 Vincent returned to Holland. Uncle Cent found his nephew another job, this time as a bookshop assistant in the town of Dordrecht. But Vincent, convinced that his vocation lay with the church, never settled down, and five months later he

left. Vincent was now determined to become a preacher, but to get a good position in the church he needed to have a university degree and, in order to enter university, he had to pass an examination in Latin and Greek. In May 1877 Vincent set off for Amsterdam, where he lived with his Uncle Jan and studied for his entrance exams. He soon felt that learning 'dead' languages was irrelevant and in July 1878 he abandoned his studies, returning to the family home in Etten.

It was then that one of Vincent's friends from England suggested a post for him. The Reverend Thomas Slade-Jones, a schoolmaster who had employed the young Dutchman in Isleworth, was visiting Holland and told him about a Belgian mission school near Brussels where academic qualifications were not required. Vincent was admitted, but after three months he failed to qualify because his teachers were convinced that he lacked the right qualities. Despite this rejection, his religious fervour was so strong that he was determined to preach the gospel. Setting off on his own, he left for the Borinage, a poverty-stricken region in the south of Belgium, and in January 1879 he obtained a six-month assignment in the coalmining village of Wasmes. There he lived like a pauper, giving away most of his clothes and sharing his food with the miners. Believing that this way of life was inappropriate for a clergyman, his superiors did not renew his contract.

Vincent refused to give up his commitment to preaching the gospel. He moved to the nearby town of Cuesmes, where he served as an evangelist without official backing from the church. For a year he lived in abject poverty, largely ignored by the mining community. Vincent suffered from intense depression: 'There may be a great fire in our soul, yet no one ever comes to warm himself at it, and the passers-by see only a wisp of smoke coming through the chimney, and go along their way,' he wrote sadly in July 1880.

Vincent's religious faith wavered but he discovered a new challenge. 'In spite of everything I shall rise again: I will take up my pencil . . . and I will go on with my drawing. From that moment everything has seemed transformed for me,' he wrote to his brother in September. In October 1880 he moved to Brussels, hoping to enrol at the Academy of Fine Art. But despite his initial enthusiasm, the transition from preacher to art student proved difficult and in April 1881 he returned to his parents' home in Etten. There he continued to practise his drawing by sketching the peasants of Brabant.

It was in Etten that Vincent fell in love again. This time the object of his affection was Kee Vos, his recently widowed cousin who had been invited to the Van Gogh home for the summer holidays. Bound up in thoughts of her lost husband, she had no idea of the deep effect she was having on her younger cousin and was astonished when Vincent suddenly declared his love. Kee immediately rejected him, in remarkably similar circumstances to the way Eugenie had reacted seven years earlier. The emptiness created by Kee's rejection killed not only Vincent's love but his remaining religious faith.

Vincent's parents found their son impossible to understand. They had been saddened when he had been sacked as an art dealer. They had found it difficult to comprehend his behaviour in the Borinage when he had given away all his possessions to the poor. Now he had fallen in love with his widowed cousin and he had rejected the church, which was taken as a personal rebuff by his father. Relations at home became increasingly tense and in November 1881 Vincent set off once again, this time returning to The Hague, where twelve years earlier he had started his career with Goupil's. Determined to learn how to paint, he convinced Theo to agree to support him financially while he developed his artistic skills.

Within a few weeks of his arrival in The Hague, Vincent fell in love with a prostitute. Sien Hoornick was struggling to bring up her five-year-old daughter by earning her living on the streets. She was pregnant, drank heavily and was very moody. Yet despite her desperate situation—or perhaps because of it—Vincent fell in love with her and transformed this 'fallen' woman into his muse.

In The Hague Vincent really began to develop his artistic skills. He asked for help from Anton Mauve, a successful painter who had married his cousin Jet Carbentus. Initially Mauve was sympathetic, encouraging him to take up painting rather than simply drawing. But Vincent was awkward to deal with and relations quickly soured. Once more Vincent was on his own, and it was then that he became interested in the English 'black-and-white' artists whose work he found in back issues of the *Illustrated London News* and the *Graphic*. Using Sien as his model, he improved his drawing and even considered returning to England to seek work as an illustrator.

Although Vincent found increasing satisfaction in his art, his relations with Sien deteriorated. She had another child, who absorbed most of her energy, and living in poverty their dream of a proper family life proved elusive. In September 1883 Vincent finally decided to break with Sien and headed for Drenthe, a desolate area in the north of the Netherlands where he wanted to paint peasant life. Here, however, with the approach of winter, conditions proved tough and lonely. After three months he gave up, reluctantly returning to his parents, who were now living in the small town of Nuenen.

Vincent spent two years in Nuenen. He painted the local peasants in earthy colours, finishing his first masterpiece, 'The Potato Eaters,' in May 1885. After his father died on 26 March 1885, Vincent found it increasingly difficult to get on with his

mother. In November he left home once more, setting off for Antwerp. He was never again to set foot in his native land.

At Antwerp Vincent enrolled at the Academy of Fine Art but, as at Brussels three years earlier, his teachers believed he had little talent. He stayed for the winter, but was impatient to move on again. By now it was clear that he would never settle down; he was destined to spend his life searching for the right place to live. Theo had chosen a different path, leading a respectable middle-class life as an art dealer. By this time he had been transferred to Paris and promoted to manager of Goupil's gallery (now renamed Boussod, Valadon & Co.) in the boulevard Montmartre.

5 VIEW FROM VINCENT'S WINDOW
Painted in the spring of 1887 from the window of the flat he shared with Theo in 54 rue Lepic, Paris.

Vincent decided to leave Antwerp to join Theo in Paris, arriving at the beginning of March 1886. Paris opened his eyes to modern art and, under the influence of the Impressionists, his colours started to become brighter. For the first time since he had been an art dealer ten years earlier he mixed with a wide range of artists, enrolling for studies at Fernand Cormon's studio and meeting some of his brother's gallery acquaintances. Vincent's list of friends from this period now reads like a roll-call of the greatest painters of the late nineteenth century: Emile Bernard, Paul Gauguin, Edgar Degas, Camille and Lucien Pissarro, Paul Signac, Georges Seurat and Henri de Toulouse-Lautrec.

Although Vincent and his brother were extremely close, they found it very difficult to live together. Vincent became increasingly restless and his thoughts turned towards a new destination. In the autumn of 1886 he wrote to the English artist Horace Livens: 'In spring—say February or even sooner—I may be going to the south of France, the land of blue tones and gay colours.'

6 THEO VAN GOGH

Recipients

THEO VAN GOGH *1857–1891*
Vincent's brother. Like Vincent he began working as an art dealer for Goupil's. He was transferred to the company's Paris gallery in 1878 and six years later he was promoted to manager of their branch at 19 boulevard Montmartre. By this time he had already begun supporting his brother financially, sending him regular allowances so that he was able to paint. In March 1886 Vincent came to stay with Theo in Paris and soon afterwards they moved into a larger flat at 54 rue Lepic. There were constant tensions between them while they were living together, and in February 1888 Vincent moved to Provence. Theo continued to send money to him there and they wrote regularly, on average twice a week. Theo visited Vincent in Provence only once, after Vincent had mutilated his ear, on Christmas Eve 1888. Vincent later stayed with Theo between 17–20 May 1890, on his way from Saint-Rémy to Auvers, and Theo and his family visited Auvers on 8 June. Theo died on 25 January 1891, six months after Vincent had taken his own life.

7 Jo Bonger

JO BONGER *1862–1925*
Theo's wife. Jo was the sister of Theo's friend Andries Bonger; she had spent her student days in London, where she studied English—specializing in the poetry of Shelley—before returning to Holland as a teacher. Theo met her briefly in Holland in the summer of 1885, again in the summer of 1887 and their relationship developed the following year. They became engaged at Christmas time and were married on 17 April 1889. Vincent met her in May 1890, on his way from Saint-Rémy to Auvers, just a

few weeks before he died. After Theo's death in 1891, Jo devoted great efforts to getting recognition for Vincent's art and had his letters published.

WIL VAN GOGH *1862–1941*
Vincent's youngest sister. She was the only one of his three sisters whom he kept in touch with when he was in Provence. Wil was then living with their elderly mother Anna, first of all in Breda and then, from the autumn of 1889, in Leiden. She was interested in art and liked to sketch. Wil also became an early member of the Dutch feminist movement. In her later life she was interned in a psychiatric asylum for many years.

8 WIL VAN GOGH

ANNA VAN GOGH *1819–1907*
Vincent's mother. His father Theodorus died on 26 March 1885 in Nuenen and after Vincent left home eight months later he never saw his mother again. She lived to the age of eighty-eight, outliving all her three sons.

9 ANNA VAN GOGH

PAUL GAUGUIN *1848–1903*
Artist. Vincent met Gauguin in Paris in November 1887, on Gauguin's return from Panama. In February 1888 Gauguin went to the Breton village of Pont-Aven to paint and then moved to Arles on 23 October. He lived with Vincent in the Yellow House, but relations between them soon became strained. After Vincent had mutilated his ear on 23 December 1888, Gauguin summoned Theo to Arles. The day after Christmas he returned to Paris with Theo. Two months later he went back to Pont-Aven. In February 1890 he returned to Paris and the following year he set off for Tahiti. He died in the Marquesas Islands.

EMILE BERNARD *1868–1941*
Artist and writer. Vincent met Bernard at Cormon's studio in Paris, in the autumn of 1886. Although he was fifteen years

younger than Vincent, they got on well. In the autumn of 1888 Bernard moved to Pont-Aven, where Gauguin was painting, and at one point he considered accompanying him to Arles. However, he returned to stay with his parents in Paris and the following summer went to Saint-Briac, on the northern coast of Brittany. Vincent and Bernard corresponded regularly, often discussing their pictures. After Vincent's death, Bernard championed his friend's work.

10 GAUGUIN
Self-portrait done for Vincent, September 1888.

11 VINCENT VAN GOGH
Portrait by John Russell, autumn 1886.

JOHN RUSSELL *1858–1931*
Australian artist. Vincent met him in Paris in the autumn of 1886 at Cormon's studio. Russell married at the beginning of 1888 and moved to Belle-Ile, in Normandy, where he painted for twenty years. Vincent wrote to him in English and two of these letters are reproduced in this book.

12 ARNOLD KONING

ARNOLD KONING *1860–1945*
Dutch artist. Koning moved into Theo's flat at 54 rue Lepic in March 1888, a few weeks after Vincent's departure, and stayed there until the end of May.

13 PAUL SIGNAC

PAUL SIGNAC *1863–1935*
French Neo-Impressionist painter. Vincent met him in Paris in 1887. They sometimes painted together at Asnières, on the northern outskirts of the city. Signac stopped at Arles for two days in March 1889, visiting Vincent on his way to the Mediterranean fishing village of Cassis.

EUGÈNE BOCH *1855–1941*
Belgian painter. In June 1888 Vincent met him at Fontvieille, a village near Arles, where Boch was staying with the American artist Dodge McKnight. Vincent painted his portrait as a 'poet', against a background of stars. In October Boch returned to the Borinage, the Belgian coalmining area where Vincent had worked as a preacher a decade earlier. In June 1890 he paid a short visit to Paris, where he met Theo and exchanged one of his pictures for one of Vincent's.

MARIE AND JOSEPH-MICHEL GINOUX *1848–1911 and 1836–1902*
The owners of the Café de la Gare in Arles. Vincent lodged with them from May to September 1888. Even after he moved into the Yellow House, which was almost next door to their café, he saw them regularly. He painted them both, and Madame Ginoux became his 'Arlésienne' as well as posing for Gauguin in October 1888, whose drawing of her is shown here. Madame Ginoux fell ill in 1889 and Vincent visited her twice from the asylum at Saint-Rémy.

14 MARIE GINOUX

15 Eugène Boch

· ARLES ·

Arles, a Roman town in the centre of Provence, was surrounded by orchards. It was here, in the strong light of the *Midi*, that Vincent escaped from the pressures of Parisian life to set up his 'studio of the South'.

16 ORCHARD IN BLOOM WITH VIEW OF ARLES
Vincent painted the peach trees just south of Arles, with the tower of Saint-Trophîme looming in the background.

17 *SKETCH OF* ORCHARD IN BLOOM WITH VIEW OF ARLES
Vincent made a little sketch of the orchard scene in a letter to his artist friend Paul Signac.

Arrival

Vincent came to Provence to find 'Japan'. In Paris he had fallen under the spell of Japanese prints, which had a strong influence on his own pictures, and he was convinced that the bright colours of the landscape in the Midi would be close to those of Japan. When he arrived, however, he did not find the Provence that he had expected as the countryside was blanketed with snow.

When Vincent's train pulled into Arles at midday on 20 February 1888, the weather was icy. Anxious to find a place to stay, he trudged through the gateway of the medieval ramparts into the old town. He needed cheap lodgings, but required a room that was large enough to work in until the weather improved. Vincent did not walk far; he stopped at the Hôtel Carrel, 30 rue Cavalerie, where he found a room on an upper floor with a view across roofs towards the centre of town.

Although the snow-covered landscape was magical, with the blossoms already in bud, the weather remained unusually cold for three weeks, forcing Vincent to work indoors. His first pictures from Provence were done inside the hotel, but he was impatient to get out into the countryside, which was not far from the centre of Arles, and as soon as the snow melted he was anxious to get out and explore. His first discovery were the orchards, where he wanted to capture the fresh blossoms against the strong blue sky. Working impatiently, as the blossom petals soon began to drop, he painted fourteen orchards in just a month.

18 THREE ORCHARDS
Above: Vincent suggested that three of his orchard pictures should be displayed as a triptych.

19 ORCHARD WITH BLOSSOMING PLUM TREES
Opposite: Once the snow melted, Vincent painted orchards with feverish excitement.

20 BLOSSOMING ALMOND BRANCH IN A GLASS
While the weather was still cold, Vincent stayed inside his hotel to paint an almond branch that was just bursting into blossom.

To Theo, 21 February 1888

My dear Theo,

During the journey I thought of you at least as much as I did of the new country I was seeing. . .

And now I'll begin by telling you that there's about two feet of snow everywhere, and more is still falling. Arles doesn't seem to me any bigger than Breda or Mons.

Before getting to Tarascon I noticed a magnificent landscape of huge yellow rocks. . . In the little village between these rocks were rows of small round trees with olive-green or grey-green leaves. . .

But here in Arles the country seems flat. I have seen some splendid red stretches of soil planted with vines, with a background of mountains of the most delicate lilac. And the landscapes in the snow, with the summits white against a sky as luminous as the snow, were just like the winter landscapes that the Japanese have painted. . .

[463] Ever yours, Vincent

21 An old woman of Arles
This is probably Vincent's first painting from Provence. The woman may well have been a member of the Carrel family, who ran the small hotel where he lodged.

To Theo, c.25 February 1888

My dear Theo,

. . . My blood is actually beginning to think of circulating, which is more than it ever did during that last period in Paris. I could not have stood it much longer. . .

Ever yours, Vincent

The studies I've done are—an old Arlésienne [21], a landscape in the snow, a view of a bit of a pavement with a pork-butcher's shop [22]. . . [464]

22 A PORK BUTCHER'S SHOP SEEN FROM A WINDOW
During the snowy weather, Vincent sat in the Carrel's restaurant and painted the view across the street.

23 DRAWBRIDGE WITH WALKING COUPLE
Above: Vincent did several paintings of the bridge, including one with a courting couple. Although he sketched this version for his friend Emile Bernard, he was dissatisfied with the painting and destroyed most of the canvas. Only the small section with the two lovers was saved.

24 DRAWBRIDGE WITH CARRIAGE
Opposite: This scene on the Canal de Bouc, on the southern outskirts of Arles, must have reminded Vincent of his native Holland.

To Theo, c.14 March 1888

MY DEAR THEO,

. . . As for my work, I brought back a size 15 canvas today. It is a drawbridge with a little cart going over it, outlined against a blue sky—the river blue as well, the banks orange with green grass and a group of women washing linen in smocks and multicoloured caps. And another landscape with a little country bridge and more women washing linen.

The weather here is changeable, often windy with murky skies, but the almond trees are beginning to flower everywhere . . .

I feel as though I were in Japan—I say no more than that, and mind, I haven't seen anything in its usual splendour yet.

That's why—even although I'm vexed that just now expenses are heavy and the pictures worthless—that's why I don't despair of the future success of this idea of a long sojourn in the Midi.

Here I am seeing new things, I am learning, and if I take it easy, my body doesn't refuse to function.

For many reasons I should like to get some sort of little retreat, where the poor cab horses of Paris—that is, you and several of our friends, the poor Impressionists—could go out to pasture when they get too beat up. . .

[469] Ever yours, Vincent

25 THE SEINE WITH THE PONT DE CLICHY
When Vincent wanted to remind Theo of one of his favourite Parisian pictures, he drew a little sketch of the bridge he had painted the previous summer.

To Bernard, 18 March 1888

MY DEAR BERNARD,

Having promised to write to you, I will begin by telling you that this country seems to me as beautiful as Japan as far as the

limpidity of the atmosphere and the gay colour effects are concerned. Water forms patches of a beautiful emerald or a rich blue in the landscape, just as we see it in the crépons [Japanese prints]. The sunsets have a pale orange colour which makes the fields appear blue. The sun a splendid yellow. And all this though I have not seen the country yet in its usual summer splendour. . .

If the Japanese are not making any progress in their own country, still it cannot be doubted that their art is being continued in France. At the top of this letter I am sending you a little scratch of a study that engrosses me, because I want to make something of it: sailors returning with their sweethearts to the town which profiles the strange silhouette of its drawbridge against an enormous yellow sun [23]. I have another study of the same drawbridge with a group of women washing [24]. . .

[B2] Sincerely yours, Vincent

26 PINK PEACH TREES
Vincent dedicated his best orchard painting to Anton Mauve, who had died on 8 February 1888. It had been Mauve, an important Dutch artist married to Vincent's cousin Jet, who had encouraged him to start painting six years earlier in The Hague.

To Wil, 30 March 1888

DEAR SISTER,

In order not to leave your letter unanswered, I will write at once after receiving your letter and Mother's, and the good wishes of you both [it was Vincent's thirty-fifth birthday]. . .

I am working on six pictures of fruit trees in bloom. And what I brought home today would probably please you—it is a dug-up square of earth in an orchard with a fence of rushes and two peach trees in full bloom. Pink against a scintillating blue sky with white clouds, and in the sunshine. It is possible you will see it, for I have finally decided to set it aside for Jet Mauve. I have written on it 'Souvenir de Mauve, Vincent & Theo' [26]. . .

You will understand that nature in the South cannot be painted

with the palette of Mauve, for instance, who belongs to the North, and who is, and will remain, a master of the grey. But at present the palette is distinctly colourful, sky blue, orange, pink, vermilion, bright yellow, bright green, bright wine-red, violet.

But by intensifying *all* the colours one arrives once again at quietude and harmony. There occurs in nature something similar to what happens in Wagner's music, which, though played by a big orchestra, is nonetheless intimate. . .

Best wishes to you and Mother, and thanks for your letters.

[W3] Vincent

27 ORCHARD SURROUNDED BY CYPRESSES
This was one of Vincent's favourite orchards, on the outskirts of Arles, and it was here that he painted the pink peach trees that he dedicated to Mauve.

To Theo, 9 April 1888

MY DEAR THEO,

Thank you for your letter and the 100-franc note enclosed. I have sent you sketches of the pictures which are to go to Holland. Of course the painted studies are more brilliant in colour. I'm hard at it again, still orchards in bloom. . .

I have another orchard, as good as the pink peach trees, apricot trees of a very pale pink. At the moment I am working on some plum trees; yellowish-white, with thousands of black branches. I am using a tremendous lot of colours and canvases, but all the same I hope it isn't a waste of money. . .

Mauve's death was a terrible blow to me. You will see that the pink peach trees were painted with a sort of passion [26].

I must also have a starry night with cypresses, or perhaps above all, a field of ripe corn; there are some wonderful nights here. I am in a continual fever of work. . .

[474] Ever yours, Vincent

28 BLOSSOMING PEAR TREE
The flowering fruit trees expressed Vincent's joy at the coming of spring. Like the other 'letter sketches', this was not intended as a polished drawing, but simply to give his friends an idea of the subjects of his latest paintings.

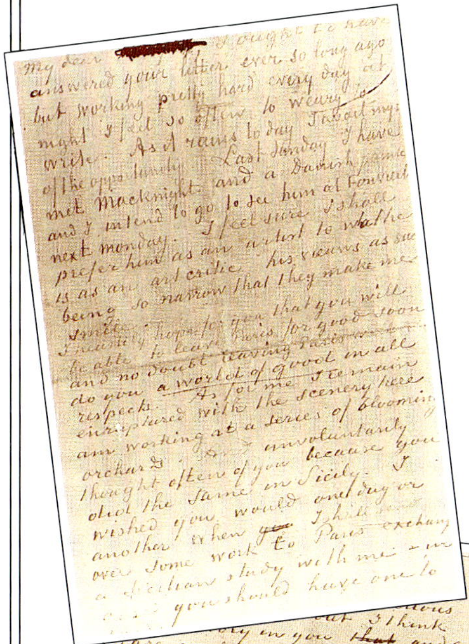

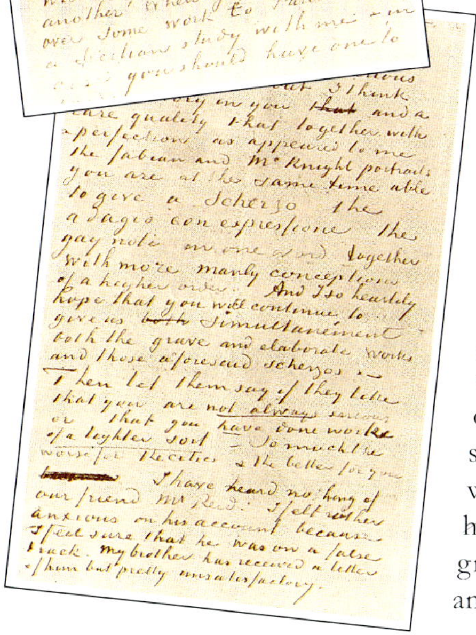

To Bernard, 9 April 1888

MY DEAR COMRADE BERNARD,

Thanks for your kind letter and for the enclosed sketches of your decoration, which I think very funny. Sometimes I regret that I cannot make up my mind to work more at home and extempore. The imagination is certainly a faculty which we must develop, one which alone can lead us to the creation of a more exalting and consoling nature than the single brief glance at reality—which in our sight is ever changing, passing like a flash of lightning—can let us perceive. . .

At the moment I am absorbed in the blooming fruit trees, pink peach trees, yellow-white pear trees. My brush stroke has no system at all. I hit the canvas with irregular touches of the brush, which I leave as they are. Patches of thickly laid-on colour, spots of canvas left uncovered, here and there portions that are left absolutely unfinished, repetitions, savageries; in short, I am inclined to think that the result is so disquieting and irritating as to be a godsend to those people who have fixed preconceived ideas about technique. . .

Working directly on the spot all the time, I try to grasp what is essential in the drawing—later I fill in the spaces which are bounded by contours—either expressed or not, but in any case *felt*—with tones which are also simplified, by which I mean that all that is going to be soil will share the same violet-like tone, that the whole sky will have a blue tint, that the green vegetation will be either green-blue or green-yellow, purposely exaggerating the yellows and blues. . .

[B3]

Your friend, Vincent

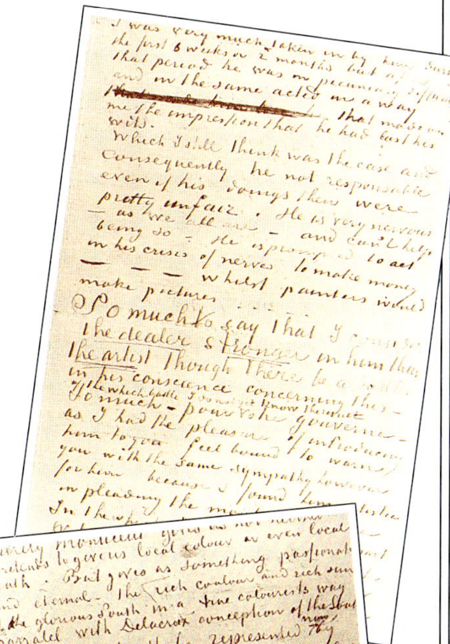

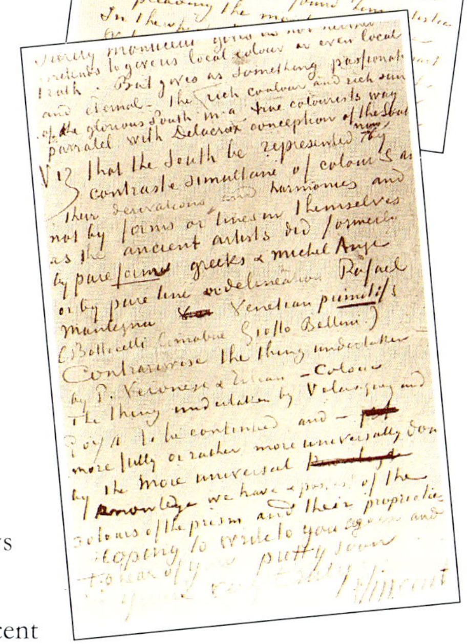

29–30 LETTER TO JOHN RUSSELL
Opposite: Vincent wrote to the Australian artist in English—evidence that he still had a good command of the language twelve years after he had left London.

To Russell, c.21 April 1888

MY DEAR RUSSELL,

I ought to have answered your letter ever so long ago, but working pretty hard every day, at night I feel so often too weary to write. As it rains today I avail myself of the opportunity. . .

I heartily hope for you that you will be able to leave Paris for good soon and no doubt leaving Paris will do you a world of good in all respects. As for me I remain enraptured with the scenery here, am working at a series of blooming orchards. . .

Hoping to write to you again and to hear of you pretty soon!

[477a] Yours very truly, Vincent

To Bernard, c. 21 April 1888

MY DEAR COMRADE BERNARD,

Many thanks for the sonnets you sent me . . . it is not as good as your painting yet; never mind, it will come; you must certainly continue your sonnets. There are so many people, especially among our comrades, who imagine that words are nothing—on the contrary, isn't it true that saying a thing well is as interesting and as difficult as painting it? There is the art of lines and colours, but the art of words is there nonetheless, and will remain.

Here is another orchard, rather simple as a composition: a white tree, a small green tree, a square patch of green, lilac soil, an orange roof, a large blue sky [31]. I am working on nine orchards: one white; one pink, almost red; one white-blue; one greyish pink; one green and pink. . .

[B4] Sincerely yours, Vincent

31 ORCHARD AND HOUSE WITH ORANGE ROOF
Vincent sketched the painting that he had done for Theo's thirty-first birthday, indicating the colours and emphasizing the orange roof standing out against the contrasting blue sky. The sketch is from the letter to Bernard.

The Yellow House

On 1 May Vincent found what he called the Yellow House, his 'studio of the South'. This small building, which had an extra bedroom for a visiting artist friend, was to become the centre of his hopes. There, he imagined, two artists could share the costs of the household and the tasks of everyday life, while supporting each other in their artistic struggles. The house was at 2 place Lamartine, just outside the medieval ramparts of the town and not far from the railway station. It looked out on a small public garden, where Vincent was often to draw and paint.

33 PUBLIC GARDEN WITH VINCENT'S HOUSE IN THE BACKGROUND
The little park became one of Vincent's favourite places, where he often drew and painted.

The Yellow House was a home where Vincent could be independent and where he had enough space to paint. He decided that he could not actually stay in his new house until he had bought some furniture and he therefore continued to sleep at the Hôtel Carrel. Unfortunately an argument developed over his bill and on 7 May he moved out, finding cheaper lodgings at the Café de la Gare at 30 place Lamartine, very close to the Yellow House.

In view of Vincent's poverty it is curious that he decided to keep a hotel room after he rented the Yellow House. It was, however, symptomatic of his somewhat impractical approach towards everyday life. He could not move into the Yellow House because it was unfurnished, but he was unable to buy furniture whilst he was having to pay his hotel bill. It nevertheless gave Vincent great pleasure to have a little house of his own.

32 VINCENT'S HOUSE
Opposite: The Yellow House became Vincent's studio. He also saw it as a home where he could welcome his fellow artists.

To Theo, 1 May 1888

MY DEAR THEO,

Many thanks for your letter and the 50-franc note enclosed. I don't see the whole future black, but I do see it bristling with difficulties and sometimes I ask myself if they won't be too much for me. But this is mostly in moments of physical weakness, and last week I had such a fierce toothache that much against my will I had to waste time.

However, I have just sent you a roll of small pen-and-ink drawings, a dozen I think. By which you will see that if I have stopped painting, I haven't stopped working. You will find among them a hasty sketch on yellow paper, a lawn in the square as you come into the town, with a building at the back, rather like this [34]. . .

Well, today I've taken the right wing of this complex, which contains 4 rooms, or rather two with two cabinets. It is painted yellow outside, whitewashed inside, on the sunny side. I have taken it for 15 francs a month. . .

I hope I have landed on my feet this time [with the new house], you know—yellow outside, white inside, with all the sun, so that I shall see my canvases in a bright interior—the floor is red brick. . .

[480] Ever yours, Vincent

34 VINCENT'S HOUSE
Vincent excitedly sketched the Yellow House for his brother, emphasizing that it symbolized a home for him by showing the front door.

To Theo, c.3 May 1888

MY DEAR THEO,

Yesterday I went to the furniture dealer's to see if I could hire a bed, etc. Unfortunately they would *not* hire, and even refused to sell on a monthly instalment plan. This is rather awkward. . .

I was certainly going the right way for a stroke when I left Paris. I paid for it nicely afterwards! When I stopped drinking, when I stopped smoking so much, when I began to think again instead of trying not to think—Good Lord, the depression and the prostration of it! Work in these magnificent natural surroundings has restored my morale, but even now some efforts are too much for me: my strength fails me. . .

If we want to live and work, we must be very sensible and look after ourselves. Cold water, fresh air, simple good food, decent clothes, a decent bed, and no women. . .

[481] Ever yours, Vincent

35 PUBLIC GARDEN WITH A CORNER OF THE YELLOW HOUSE
A drawing of the small park in the centre of the place Lamartine.

To Theo, c.4 May 1888

MY DEAR THEO,

. . . It is a filthy town this, with the old streets. As for the women of Arles. . . [they] are. . . no longer what they must have been. . .

I shall go on working and here and there among my work there will be things which will last, but who will be in figure painting what Claude Monet is in landscape? However, you must feel, as I do, that such a one will come. Rodin? He does not work in colour, he's not the one. But the painter of the future will be *a colourist such as has never yet existed.* Manet was working toward it, but as you know the Impressionists have already got a stronger colour than Manet. But this painter who is to come—I can't imagine him living in little cafés, working away with a lot of false teeth, and going to the Zouaves' [soldiers] brothels, as I do. . .

[482] Ever yours, Vincent

36 FARMHOUSE WITH WHEATFIELD ALONG A ROAD AND FIELD WITH FLOWERS
The upper sketch is of a painting Vincent did beside the road to Tarascon. The lower one shows the composition of the picture of irises with the distant church towers of Arles [frontispiece].

To Theo, 12 May 1888

MY DEAR THEO,

. . . I have done two new studies like these: you have a drawing of one of them already, a farm by the high road among cornfields [36]. A meadow full of very yellow buttercups, a ditch with irises, green leaves and purple flowers, the town in the background, some grey willows, and a strip of blue sky [frontispiece].

If the meadow does not get mowed, I'd like to do this study again, for the subject was very beautiful, and I had some trouble getting the composition. A little town surrounded by fields all covered with yellow and purple flowers; exactly—can't you see it?—like a Japanese dream. . .

With a handshake, write soon
Ever yours, Vincent

[487]

To Theo, c.20 May 1888

MY DEAR THEO,

. . . I am doing very well down here, but it is because I have my work here, and nature, and if I didn't have that, I should grow melancholy. If work had any attraction for you where you are, and if the Impressionists were getting on, it would be a very good thing. For loneliness, worries, difficulties, the unsatisfied need for kindness and sympathy—that is what is hard to bear. . .

I have done two still lifes this week.

A blue enamel coffeepot, a cup (on the left), royal blue and gold, a milk jug in squares of pale blue and white, a cup—on the right—of white with a blue and orange pattern, on an earthen tray of greyish yellow, a jug in earthenware or majolica, blue with a

37 The road to Tarascon with a man walking
One of Vincent's favourite walks was the road north from the place Lamartine towards Tarascon. The striding figure could be a self-portrait.

pattern in reds, greens and browns, and lastly two oranges and three lemons; the table is covered with a blue cloth, the background is greenish-yellow, so that there are six different blues and four or five yellows and oranges [38].

The other still life is the majolica pot with wild flowers. . .

In the fullness of artistic life there is, and remains, and will always come back at times, that homesick longing for the truly ideal life that can never come true.

And sometimes you lack all desire to throw yourself heart and soul into art, and to get well for that. You know you are a cab horse and that it's the same old cab you'll be hitched up to again: that you'd rather live in a meadow with the sun, a river and other horses for company, likewise free, and the act of procreation. . .

I do not know who it was who called this condition—being struck by death and immortality. The cab you drag along must be of some use to people you do not know. And so, if we believe in the new art and in the artists of the future, our faith does not cheat us. When good old Corot said a few days before his death—'Last

night in a dream I saw landscapes with skies all pink,' well, haven't they come, those skies all pink, and yellow and green into the bargain, in the Impressionist landscapes? All of which means that there are things one feels coming, and they are coming in very truth.

And as for us who are not, I am inclined to believe, nearly so close to death, we nevertheless feel that this thing is greater than we are, and that its life is of longer duration than ours.

We do not feel we are dying, but we do feel the truth that we are of small account, and that we are paying a hard price to be a link in the chain of artists, in health, in youth, in liberty, none of which we enjoy, any more than the cab horse that hauls a coachful of people out to enjoy the spring. . .

[489] Ever yours, Vincent

38 Still life with coffee pot
Vincent was able to take his breakfast at the Yellow House although he slept in his hotel. This is a sketch of the painting he made to celebrate his new home, with the colours marked to show his use of complementaries.

To Bernard, c.20 May 1888

My dear Bernard,

. . . My dear comrade, I should have written you before, only I had a lot of things to attend to. . .

What have you painted recently? As for me, I have done a still life [38]. . .

Then I have another still life, lemons in a basket against a yellow background.

Further a view of Arles. Of the town itself one sees only some red roofs and a tower, the rest is hidden by the green foliage of fig trees, far away in the background, and a narrow strip of blue sky above it. The town is surrounded by immense meadows all abloom with countless buttercups—a sea of yellow—in the foreground these meadows are divided by a ditch full of violet irises. They were mowing the grass while I was painting, so it is only a study

39 View of Arles from a hill
This was drawn from the ruins of the Benedictine abbey of Montmajour, looking across the reclaimed marshland of the Crau towards Arles. It was the last of a series of eight drawings that Vincent did at Montmajour in May.

and not the finished picture that I had intended to do. But what a subject, isn't it! That sea of yellow with a band of violet irises, and in the background that coquettish little town of the pretty women! [frontispiece]. Then two studies of roadsides. . .

[B5] Vincent

To Theo, 28 May 1888

My dear Theo,

. . . You know what you must do with these drawings—make sketchbooks with 6 or 10 or 12 like those books of original Japanese drawings. *I very much want* to make such a book for Gauguin, and one for Bernard. For the drawings are going to be better than these [40]. . .

[492] Ever yours, Vincent

40 Vincent's projected sketchbook
Vincent wanted the drawings he had done in his first weeks in Arles to be collected together. Among the subjects he thought should be included was his farmhouse on the Tarascon road [36], a landscape with a tree, the ruins of Montmajour and the drawbridge.

To Theo, 28 May 1888

My dear Theo,

I have been thinking about Gauguin, and look here. If Gauguin wants to come here, there is Gauguin's journey, and there are two beds or two mattresses, which in that case we absolutely must buy. But afterwards, as Gauguin is a sailor, we shall probably manage to eat at home.

And the two of us will live on the same money that I now spend by myself.

You know that I have always thought it idiotic the way painters live alone, etc. You always lose by being isolated. . .

[493] Ever yours, Vincent

To the Sea

Vincent's only visit to the Mediterranean was the five-day trip that he made to the fishing village of Saintes-Maries-de-la-Mer. He left by diligence early in the morning of 30 May and arrived at midday. His first major excursion outside Arles must have been exciting as the journey took him across the marshland of the Camargue, with its wild horses and sea birds. He was full of anticipation on seeing the church tower of Saintes-Maries stand out against the flat landscape.

41 BEACH, SEA AND FISHING BOATS
Vincent drew the boats from behind sand dunes.

For Vincent, who had only known the dark waters of the North Sea, the strong colours of the Mediterranean made a powerful impression. He came to paint, not for a holiday, and brought with him three pieces of canvas, which he finished, and plenty of paper for sketches. Although he had planned to leave on 2 June, he stayed for an extra day and he returned to Arles with nine completed drawings. These were to provide the inspiration for a further series of paintings that he did back at his studio in the Yellow House.

42 *SKETCH OF* FISHING BOATS ON THE BEACH

The Mediterranean was to have a deep influence on Vincent's work. The strong light excited him, giving him confidence to explore the effects that he could achieve through using complementary colours—blues and oranges, purples and yellows, and greens and reds. The short length of Vincent's stay meant he had to work at great speed. He exaggerated what he saw and his pictures assumed a new spontaneity.

43 FISHING BOATS ON THE BEACH
Opposite: This picture was painted on Vincent's return to Arles. The four boats out at sea echo the four on the beach.

AMITIE

44 VIEW OF
SAINTES-MARIES

This was what Vincent saw when he arrived at the village after a five-hour trip across the Camargue by horse-drawn carriage. The mauve lavender fields and the church dominate the composition.

To Theo, 29 May 1888

My dear Theo,

. . . Early tomorrow I start for Saintes-Maries on the Mediterranean. I shall stay there till Saturday evening.

I am taking two canvases, but I'm rather afraid it will probably be too windy to paint.

You go by diligence, it is 50 kilometres from here. You cross the Camargue, grass plains where there are herds of fighting bulls and also herds of little white horses, half wild and very beautiful.

I am taking especially whatever I need for drawing. I must draw a great deal, for the very reason you spoke of in your last letter. Things here have so much line. And I want to get my drawing more spontaneous, more exaggerated. . .

[495] Ever yours, Vincent

To Theo, c.2 June 1888

My dear Theo,

I am at last writing to you from Saintes-Maries on the shore of the Mediterranean. The Mediterranean has the colours of mackerel, changeable I mean. You don't always know if it is green or violet, you can't even say it's blue, because the next moment the changing light has taken on a tinge of pink or grey. . .

One night I went for a walk by the sea along the empty shore. It was not gay, but neither was it sad—it was—beautiful. The deep blue sky was flecked with clouds of a blue deeper than the fundamental blue of intense cobalt, and others of a clearer blue,

45 Woman with chequered dress
This little sketch was to explain the effect of black and white contrasting with blue and orange.

like the blue whiteness of the Milky Way. In the blue depth the stars were sparkling, greenish, yellow, white, pink, more brilliant, more sparklingly gemlike than at home—even in Paris: opals you might call them, emeralds, lapis lazuli, rubies, sapphires. The sea was very deep ultramarine—the shore a sort of violet and faint russet as I saw it, and on the dunes (they are about seventeen feet high) some bushes Prussian blue.

46 *SKETCH OF* STREET IN SAINTES-MARIES

Besides half-page drawings I have a big drawing, the pendant of the last one. Good-bye for the present only, I hope, with a handshake,

[499] Ever yours, Vincent

To Theo, c. 4 June 1888

MY DEAR THEO,

. . . Now that I have seen the sea here, I am absolutely convinced of the importance of staying in the Midi, and of positively piling it on, exaggerating the colour—Africa not so far away. I am sending you by the same post the drawings of Saintes-Maries. I made the sketch of the boats just as I was going to start in the morning, very early, and I am working on the picture after it, a size 30 canvas with more sea and sky on the right [43].

It was before the boats cleared off; I had watched it all the other mornings, but as they leave very early, I didn't have time to do it. . .

I wish you could spend some time here, you would feel it after a while, one's sight changes: you see things with an eye more Japanese, you feel colour differently. The Japanese draw quickly, very quickly, like a lightning flash. . .

I am convinced that I shall set my individuality free simply by staying on here.

I have only been here a few months, but tell me this—could I, in Paris, have done the drawing of the boats *in an hour?*. . .

What Pissarro says is true, you must boldly exaggerate the effects of either harmony or discord which colours produce. It is the same as in drawing—accurate drawing, accurate colour, is perhaps not the essential thing to aim at, because the reflection of reality in a mirror, if it could be caught, colour and all, would not be a picture at all, no more than a photograph.

Good-bye for the present. . .

[500] Ever yours, Vincent

47 Street in Saintes-Maries
Vincent painted this masterly composition, based on the contrast of complementary colours, on his return to Arles.

To Bernard, c. 5 June 1888

My dear comrade Bernard,

. . .Imagine. . . a cottage whitewashed all over (the roof too) standing in an orange field—certainly orange, for the southern sky and the blue Mediterranean provoke an orange tint that gets more intense as the scale of blue colours gets a more vigorous tone—then the black note of the door, the windows and the little cross on the ridge of the roof produce a simultaneous contrast of black and white just as pleasing to the eye as that of blue and orange [48].

Or let us take a more amusing motif: imagine a woman in a black-and-white checked dress in the same primitive landscape with a blue sky and an orange soil [45]. . .

[B6] Sincerely yours, Vincent

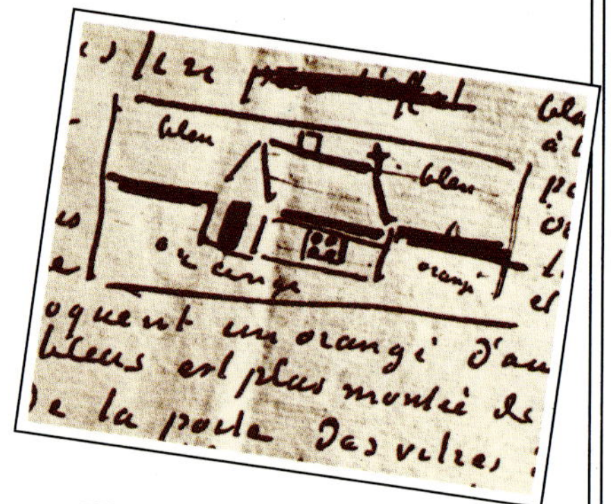

48 Whitewashed cottage
This little sketch was done to show the contrast between the strong Mediterranean sky and the field, which is tinged orange by the intensity of the blue sky.

Harvest

50 SKETCH OF WHEATFIELD WITH SETTING SUN
Vincent sketched the field, with the distant view of Arles, for his friend Bernard.

49 HARVEST LANDSCAPE
Opposite: This was the first large picture that Vincent did in Provence and he believed it to be his best work of the summer. Painted in the Crau, the ruins of the abbey of Montmajour are visible on the left of the horizon.

A few days after his return from Saintes-Maries-de-la-Mer Vincent found a new subject, the harvest. He took his canvases out into the fields, just outside Arles, and worked as hard as the farmers who were taking in the wheat. In just one week, he finished ten paintings. For Vincent, who had painted the peasants of Brabant at work, the gathering of the harvest reminded him of his early artistic endeavours. The changing seasons made a deep impression on him, as he felt they symbolized the cycle of human life.

Vincent's harvest paintings were done in the Crau, an area of low-lying, reclaimed marshland to the east of Arles. The Crau began close to the town, just a few minutes' walk away from the Yellow House, and it ran up to the foothills of the Alpilles. Vincent loved to walk to these hills, particularly to the ruined abbey of Montmajour, and then look back across the wheatfields to the distant town of Arles.

The yellowing wheat against a blue sky was visually an exciting subject for Vincent. And, as he trudged over the fields, under the beating sun, he was struck by the contrasts he found in the landscape: between the countryside and the town of Arles in the distance, between farming and industry and in the figure of an isolated reaper in a vast field. The resulting series of harvest scenes, although painted at a hectic pace, proved to be among his most powerful landscapes.

51 WHEATFIELD WITH SETTING SUN
In the background is a mixture of old and new in the town: Vincent has included the arches of the Roman arena, the church towers of Arles, a railway train and smoking factory chimneys.

52 Girl's head
Vincent drew this portrait by the banks of the Rhône and sent it to his Australian friend Russell.

To Russell, c.17 June 1888

My dear Russell,

For ever so long I have been wanting to write you—but then the work has so taken me up. We have harvest time here at present and I am always in the fields.

And when I sit down to write I am so abstracted by recollections of what I have seen that I leave the letter. . .

Well, instead of continuing the letter I began to draw on the very paper the head of the dirty little girl I saw this afternoon whilst I was painting a view of the river with a greenish yellow sky [52]. . .

My brother has an exhibition of 10 new pictures by Claude Monet—his latest works . . . I wished I could see them. . .

Am working at a 'Sower': the great field all violet, the sky & sun very yellow, it is a hard subject to treat.

Please remember me very kindly to Mrs Russell—and in thought I heartily shake hands.

[501a] Yours very truly, Vincent

To Bernard, c.18 June 1888

My dear Bernard,

. . . I feel much better here than I did in the North. I work even in the middle of the day, in the full sunshine, without any shadow at all, in the wheatfields, and I enjoy it like a cicada. My God, if I had only known this country at the age of twenty-five, instead of coming here when I was thirty-five years old!. . .

Here is a sketch of a sower: large ploughed field with clods of earth, for the most part frankly violet. . .

My dear for ever so long I have
been wanting to write to you - but then
the work has so taken me up. We have
harvest time here at present and I am
always in the fields.
And when I sit down to write I
am so abstracted by recollections of
what I have seen that I leave the
letter. For instance at the present
occasion I was writing to you and
going to say something about Arles
as it is - and as it was in the
old days of Boccaccio. -
Well instead of continuing the letter
I began to draw on the very paper
the head of a dirty little girl I saw
this afternoon whilst I was painting
a view of the greenish yellow

I heard Rodin had a beautiful
head at the Salon.
I have been to the seaside for a
week and very likely am going thither
again soon. - Flat shore
sands - fine figures there
like Cimabue - straight stylish.
Am working at a Sower.

the great field all violet the sky & sun very
yellow. it is a hard subject to treat.
Please remember me very kindly to
Mrs Russell - and in thought I heartily
shake hands. Yours very truly
Vincent

53 Letter to Russell
Vincent's handwriting reveals an astonishing range of styles here, changing all the time and reflecting the mood of what he is saying.

54 SOWER WITH SETTING SUN
Sowing was not done until the autumn, but Vincent did this painting during the harvest. The figure was inspired by the famous 'Sower' of the French artist Millet.

There are many hints of yellow in the soil, neutral tones resulting from mixing violet with yellow; but I have played hell somewhat with the truthfulness of the colours [54]. . .

I won't hide from you that I don't dislike the country, as I have been brought up there—I am still charmed by the magic of hosts of memories of the past, of a longing for the infinite, of which the sower, the sheaf are the symbols—just as much as before. But when shall I paint my *starry sky*, that picture which preoccupies me continuously? . . . Herewith another landscape. Sunset? Rising moon? In any case a summer sun. The town violet, the orb yellow, the sky blue-green. The wheat has all the tones of old gold, copper, gold-green or gold-red, gold-yellow, bronze-yellow, green-red. Size 30 canvas, square [49]. . .

[B7] A handshake, Vincent

To Theo, 21 June 1888

My dear Theo,

. . .I have a model at last—a Zouave—a boy with a small face, a bull neck, and the eye of a tiger, and I began with one portrait, and began again with another; the half-length I did of him was horribly harsh, in a blue uniform, the blue of enamel saucepans, with braids of a faded reddish-orange, and two stars on his breast, an ordinary blue, and very hard to do. That bronzed, feline head of his with the reddish cap, against a green door and the orange bricks of a wall [55]. So it's a savage combination of incongruous tones, not easy to manage. The study I made of it seems to me very harsh, but all the same I'd like always to be working on vulgar, even loud portraits like this. It teaches me something, and above all that is what I want of my work. . .

[501] Ever yours, Vincent

55 Zouave, half-figure
Vincent painted the soldier of the Zouave regiment inside the Yellow House, during heavy rains at the end of June.

56 Newly mown lawn with weeping tree
A sketch of the first painting Vincent did in the public garden in front of the Yellow House.

To Bernard, 24 June 1888

My dear Bernard,

. . .How tired you get in the sun here! In the same way I am wholly unable to judge my own work. I cannot see whether the studies are good or bad. I have seven studies of wheatfields, all of them landscapes unfortunately, very much against my will. The landscapes yellow—old gold—done quickly, quickly, quickly and in a hurry, just like the harvester who is silent under the blazing sun, intent only on his reaping. . .

[B9] Yours sincerely, Vincent

To Theo, c.5 July 1888

My dear Theo,

. . . Here is a new subject. A corner or a garden with clipped shrubs and a weeping tree, and in the background some clumps of oleanders. And the lawn just cut with long trails of hay drying in the sun, and a little corner of blue sky at the top [56]. . .

Often whole days pass without my speaking to anyone, except to ask for dinner or coffee. And it has been like that from the beginning.

But up to now the loneliness has not worried me much because I have found the brighter sun and its effect on nature so absorbing.

Write me a day or two early if you can, the end of the week will be rather tough.

[508] Ever yours, Vincent

57 Landscape with Alphonse Daudet's windmill
The windmill, just outside the village of Fontvieille, had been immortalized in Daudet's novel Lettres de mon Moulin.

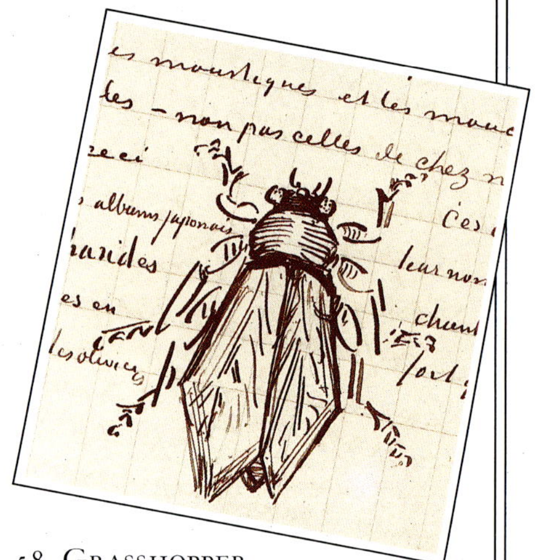

58 Grasshopper
Vincent was surrounded by noisy grasshoppers when he painted the summer harvest scenes.

To Theo, c.9 July 1888

My dear Theo,

I have come back from a day in Montmajour, and my friend the second lieutenant [Milliet] was with me. We explored the old garden together, and stole some excellent figs. If it had been bigger, it would have made me think of Zola's Paradou, high reeds, and vines, ivy, fig trees, olives, pomegranates with lusty flowers of the brightest orange, hundred-year-old cypresses, ash trees, and willows, rock oaks, half-broken flights of steps, ogive windows in ruins, blocks of white rock covered with lichen, and scattered fragments of crumbling walls among the green. . .

59 LANDSCAPE NEAR MONTMAJOUR WITH TRAIN
This was drawn just west of the abbey, looking towards the Rhône. Along with the train, Vincent has also included a horse-and-cart and two walkers.

I brought back another big drawing, but not of the garden. That makes three drawings. When I have half a dozen I shall send them along...

I think the heat is still doing me good, in spite of the mosquitoes and flies.

The grasshoppers—not like ours at home, but like those you see in Japanese sketchbooks, and Spanish flies, gold and green in swarms on the olives. The grasshoppers (I think they are called cicadas) sing as loud as a frog...

A handshake,

[506] Ever yours, Vincent

To Theo, c.13 July 1888

MY DEAR THEO,

...In my opinion the two views of the Crau and of the country on the banks of the Rhône are the best things I have done in pen and ink...

The fascination that these huge plains have for me is very strong, so that I felt no *weariness*, in spite of the really wearisome circumstances, mistral and mosquitoes. If a view makes you forget these little annoyances, it must have something in it. You will see, however, that there is no attempt at effect. At first sight it is like a map, a strategic plan as far as the *execution* goes. Besides, I walked there *with a painter*, and he said, 'There is something that would be boring to paint.' Yet I went fully fifty times to Montmajour to look at this flat landscape, and was I wrong? I went for a walk there with someone else who was *not a painter* [probably Milliet], and when I said to him, 'Look, to me that is as beautiful and as infinite as the sea,' he said—and he

60 HILL WITH THE RUINS OF MONTMAJOUR
A view of the fourteenth-century tower of the ruined Benedictine abbey.

knows the sea—'For my part I like this *better* than the sea, because it is no less infinite, and yet you feel that it is *inhabited*.'

What a picture I would make of it if there was not this damn wind. That is the maddening thing here, no matter where you set up your easel. And that is largely why the painted studies are not so finished as the drawings; the canvas is shaking all the time. . .

[509] Ever yours, Vincent

61 *SKETCH OF* GARDEN WITH FLOWERS
Vincent's sketch in a letter to Theo.

To Bernard, 15 July 1888

MY DEAR COMRADE BERNARD,

. . . I have done some large pen-and-ink drawings. . . an immense stretch of flat country, a bird's-eye view of it seen from the top of a hill—vineyards and fields of newly reaped wheat. All this multiplied in endless repetitions. . . a microscopic figure of a labourer, a little train running across the wheatfield—this is all the animation there is in it [59]. . .

[B10] Sincerely yours, Vincent

62 GARDEN WITH SUNFLOWERS
Vincent's drawing anticipates his series of glorious sunflower paintings. He signed the picture on the bucket.

To Theo, 8 August 1888

MY DEAR THEO,

The one with the sunflowers is a little garden of a bathing establishment [62]. . .

Under the blue sky the orange, yellow, red splashes of the flowers take on an amazing brilliance, and in the limpid air there is a something or other happier, more lovely than in the North. . .

[519] Ever yours, Vincent

Sunflowers

Nothing symbolizes Vincent's feeling for Provence more than his paintings of sunflowers. The flowers represented the sun, the dominant feature of summer in the Midi. Vincent began to paint the sunflowers with a very special purpose in mind, to decorate the room of his friend Paul Gauguin, who he hoped would soon join him. Gauguin, then painting in Brittany, had talked of coming to Provence, but he kept delaying his departure on the grounds of ill-health and poverty.

Gauguin was a friend of Theo's, and Vincent had got to know him in Paris. Vincent, who admired his work and wanted his encouragement, was now desperate that he should come. He had few artist friends in Arles and after his time in Paris, when he was constantly mixing with other painters, he felt isolated. In addition Vincent had financial problems, partly because he had little idea about managing money, and he was convinced, rather naively, that it would be more economical to live with a companion.

As the summer wore on, Vincent became increasingly anxious that Gauguin should join him in Provence. In the meantime, as he waited, he painted a series of pictures to decorate the room of the artist he believed should come and lead the 'studio of the South'. These paintings are among his finest work.

63 SUNFLOWERS
Two years after he had painted his sunflower series, Vincent made several sketches of the image that had captured his imagination.

64 FOURTEEN SUNFLOWERS IN A VASE
For Vincent, yellow was a symbol of hope and friendship.

65 TWELVE SUNFLOWERS IN A VASE
A few weeks later Gauguin was to do a portrait of Vincent working on a sunflower painting.

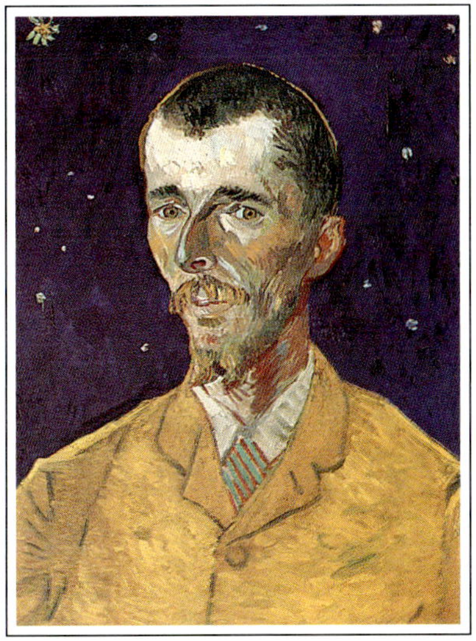

66 PORTRAIT OF EUGÈNE BOCH
The Belgian artist was visiting Vincent's friend Dodge MacKnight, an American painter who was staying in Fontvieille.

To Bernard, c.18 August 1888

MY DEAR BERNARD,

. . . Oh! that beautiful midsummer sun here. It beats down on one's head, and I haven't the slightest doubt that it makes one crazy. But as I was so to begin with, I only enjoy it.

I am thinking of decorating my studio with half a dozen pictures of 'Sunflowers', a decoration in which the raw or broken chrome yellows will blaze forth on various backgrounds. . .

[B15] Sincerely yours, Vincent

To Theo, 3 September 1888

MY DEAR THEO,

. . . I at last have a first sketch of that picture which I have dreamed of for so long—the poet. He posed for me. His fine head with that keen gaze stands out in my portrait against a starry sky of deep ultramarine; for clothes, a short yellow coat, a collar of unbleached linen, and a spotted tie [66]. . .

[531] Ever yours, Vincent

67 CAFÉ TERRACE AT NIGHT
This was Vincent's first outdoor 'night' painting. The Grand Café was in the Place du Forum, the main square in the centre of Arles.

To Theo, 8 September 1888

MY DEAR THEO,

. . . The picture ['The Night Café'] is one of the ugliest I have done [68]. It is the equivalent, though different, of the 'Potato Eaters'.

68 THE NIGHT CAFÉ
The Café de la Gare, where Vincent lodged with the Ginoux family from May until September 1888.

69 SELF-PORTRAIT WITH STRAW HAT AND PIPE
Vincent is wearing his painting smock and the hat he used to protect himself against the sun.

I have tried to express the terrible passions of humanity by means of red and green.

The room is blood red and dark yellow with a green billiard table in the middle; there are four citron-yellow lamps with a glow of orange and green. Everywhere there is a clash and contrast of the most disparate reds and greens in the figures of little sleeping hooligans, in the empty, dreary room, in violet and blue. The blood-red and the yellow-green of the billiard table, for instance, contrast with the soft tender Louis XV green of the counter, on which there is a pink nosegay. The white coat of the landlord, awake in a corner of that furnace, turns citron-yellow, or pale luminous green. . .

[533] Ever yours, Vincent

At Home

On 16 September 1888 Vincent slept at the Yellow House for the first time. Although he had started renting the house more than four months earlier, it was only when Theo sent him 300 francs from a family legacy at the beginning of September that he was able to furnish his new home. He was still awaiting the arrival of Gauguin and was anxious to tell him that everything was ready, having spent much time and effort to make the house as comfortable as possible, in spite of limited funds. He tells Gauguin that he has had gas lighting installed, and writes to Theo about the paintings he has done to decorate Gauguin's room.

In spite of his domestic chores, Vincent continued to paint with furious energy. The range of subjects that he chose in the few weeks before Gauguin's arrival is astonishing. He often drew and painted in the public garden that lay just in front of the Yellow House. He walked along the banks of the Rhône, 'capturing' a night scene under a starry sky. He painted portraits of his friends. (So keen was he to see his new work framed that he overspent his allowance and had to survive for four days on nothing but cups of coffee and a little bread.) Finally, just before Gauguin's arrival, Vincent did a painting of his bedroom, confirming that the Yellow House had become his home—and a refuge for his fellow artists.

71 VINCENT'S BEDROOM
When Vincent sketched his bedroom for Theo (left [70]), he had hung a portrait of his mother [79] on the wall, but when he did the painting the next day he had changed his mind and replaced it with a landscape.

To Theo, c.27 September 1888

My dear Theo,

I know quite well that I have already written to you once today, but it has been such a lovely day again. My great regret is that you cannot see what I am seeing here.

72 A lane in the public garden
Vincent called the small park in front of the Yellow House the 'poet's garden' in honour of Petrarch, the fourteenth-century poet who had lived in Provence. The figure on the far right with the blue coat and yellow hat could be a self-portrait.

Since seven o'clock this morning I have been sitting in front of something which after all is no great matter, a clipped round bush of cedar or cypress growing amid grass. You already know this clipped bush, because you have had a study of the garden. Enclosed also a sketch of my canvas [73], again a square size 30.

73 Round clipped shrub in the public garden
This is the drawing that Vincent sent to Theo; it is based on a painting that has disappeared. Vincent was intrigued by this bush, which he included in a number of his pictures.

The bush is green, touched a little with bronze and various other tints.

The grass is bright, bright green, malachite touched with citron, and the sky is bright, bright blue.

The row of bushes in the background are all oleanders, raving mad; the blasted things are flowering so riotously they may well catch locomotor ataxia. They are loaded with fresh flowers, and quantities of faded flowers as well, and their green is continually renewing itself in fresh, strong shoots, apparently inexhaustibly.

A funereal cypress is standing over them, and some small figures are sauntering along a pink path. . .

Milliet today was pleased with what I had done—the 'Ploughed Field'; generally he does not like what I do, but because the colour of the lumps of earth is as soft as a pair of sabots, it did not offend him, with the forget-me-not blue sky flecked with white clouds. If he posed better, he would give me great pleasure, and he would have a more distinctive portrait than I can manage now, though the subject is good—the matt pale tints of his face, the red

soldier's cap against an emerald background [74]. Oh, how I wish you could see all that I am seeing these days. I can only let myself go with so many lovely things in front of me, especially as I think that the work is getting somewhat better . . .

[541] Ever yours, Vincent

To Theo,* c.*29 September 1888

74 Lieutenant Milliet
Paul-Eugène Milliet had recently returned from French Indochina. Vincent became friends with him and tried to teach him to paint.

My dear Theo,

. . . Enclosed a little sketch of a square size 30 canvas, the starry sky actually painted at night under a gas jet. The sky is greenish-blue, the water royal blue, the ground mauve. The town is blue and violet, the gas is yellow and the reflections are russet-gold down to greenish-bronze. On the blue-green expanse of sky the Great Bear sparkles green and pink, its discreet pallor contrasts with the harsh gold of the gas [75].

Also a sketch of a size 30 canvas representing the house and its surroundings in sulphur-coloured sunshine, under a sky of pure cobalt. The subject is frightfully difficult; but that is just why I want to conquer it. It's terrific, these houses, yellow in the sun, and the incomparable freshness of the blue. And everywhere the ground is yellow too [320. I shall send you a better drawing than this rough improvised sketch out of my head later on.

The house on the left is pink with green shutters, I mean the one in the shadow of the tree. That is the restaurant where I go for dinner every day. My friend the postman lives at the end of the street on the left, between the two railway bridges. The night café I painted is not in the picture, it is to the left of the restaurant. . .

[543] Ever yours, Vincent

76 *Sketch of* The starry night
Vincent's sketch, for his friend Boch, emphasizes the bright stars which rise above the street lights along the riverside.

75 The starry night
Opposite: A view of the Rhône from the edge of the place Lamartine, with a couple strolling along the bank in the foreground and the lights of the town in the distance. Vincent's heightened mood found expression in this majestic painting.

To Boch, 2 October 1888

My dear friend Boch,

. . . Now I must tell you a piece of news, namely that I have furnished the house at last and that I have immediately furnished a bedroom for Gauguin or for anyone who should come.

The house is a lot brighter now that it is furnished. After that I have worked like blazes, for the autumn is without wind and superb. I am also working on seven square size 30 canvases. In the first place the night café where I have stayed with lamplight effect, painted in the night-time [68].

Three views of the public garden in front of the house.

This is one of these views. A cypress or cedar shrub in a bottle-green tub on a citron-hued green lawn. In the background a row of oleanders and two statuettes. The sky a raw cobalt blue. You see, it is even a lot simpler than formerly.

Then ploughed fields; a scenery with nothing but lumps of earth, the furrows the colour of an old wooden shoe under a forget-me-not blue sky with white cloud flocks.

Further a view of my house and its surroundings in a sulphur sun. The sky a hard and bright cobalt. A difficult job, I tell you! [32].

Then a view of the café on Forum Square where we used to go, *painted by night* [67].

And lastly a study of the Rhône—of the town lighted with gas reflected in the blue river [75 & 76].

Over it the starry sky with the Great Bear—a sparkling of pink and green on the cobalt blue field of the night sky, whereas the lights of the town and its ruthless reflections are red gold and bronzed green.

The garden with the oleanders and the shrub in a tub has an impasto like painted porcelain.

77 Envelope addressed to Eugène Boch
Vincent frequently misspelled names: here he addressed his friend as 'Bock' and gave him the initial 'F'.

Your portrait is in my bedroom [66] along with that of Milliet, the Zouave, which I have just finished [74]. . .

A hearty handshake and good courage and a lot of success with your work.

[553b] Sincerely, Vincent

Excuse my great hurry; I haven't even time to read this letter over. . .

78 SELF-PORTRAIT
Vincent presented this picture to Gauguin, inscribed 'à mon ami Paul G'. This dedication was later partly removed by Gauguin, but whether he defaced the inscription deliberately or by mistake remains a mystery.

To Gauguin, 3 October 1888

MY DEAR GAUGUIN,

. . . When I left Paris, seriously sick at heart and in body, and nearly an alcoholic because of my rising fury at my strength failing me—then I shut myself up within myself, without having the courage to hope!

Now, however, hope is breaking for me vaguely on the horizon; that hope in intermittent flashes, like a lighthouse, which has sometimes comforted me during my solitary life.

And now I am longing so much to give you a large share in that faith . . .

These days I have an extraordinary feverish energy; at the moment I am struggling with a landscape that has a blue sky over an immense vine, green, purple, yellow, with black and orange branches. Little figures of ladies with red sunshades and of vintagers with their cart enliven it even more. In the foreground, grey sand. Yet another square size 30 canvas for the adornment of the house.

I have a portrait of myself, all ash-coloured. The ashen-grey colour that is the result of mixing malachite green with an orange hue, on pale malachite ground, all in harmony with the reddish-brown clothes. But as I also exaggerate my personality, I have in

the first place aimed at the character of a simple bronze worshipping the Eternal Buddha [78]. . .

[544a] Ever yours, Vincent

To Theo, 8 October 1888

My dear Theo,

Thanks for your letter, but I have had a very thin time of it these days, as my money ran out on Thursday, so it was a damnably long time till Monday noon. These four days I have lived mainly on 23 cups of coffee, with bread which I still have to pay for. It's not your fault, it's mine if it's anyone's. Because I was wild to see my pictures in frames, and I had ordered too many for my budget, seeing that the month's rent and the charwoman also had to be paid. And even today is going to drain me dry, because I must also buy some canvas . . .

I venture to think that if you saw the studies, you would say I was right to work at white heat as long as it was fine. It wasn't so the last few days, there is a merciless mistral furiously sweeping along the dead leaves. But between now and the winter there will be another spell of magnificent weather and magnificent effects, and then the thing will be to make another headlong spurt. I am so much taken up with the work that I cannot come to a dead stop. . .

I am doing a portrait of Mother for myself. I cannot stand the colourless photograph, and I am trying to do one in a harmony of colour, as I see her in my memory [79].

A good handshake.

[546] Ever yours, Vincent

79 Portrait of Vincent's mother
This was painted from a photograph Vincent had just received of his mother Anna.

To Theo, 13 October 1888

My dear Theo,

80 The Tarascon stagecoach
Vincent liked Daudet's novel Tartarin de Tarascon, *about a horse-drawn carriage that ends up in North Africa, and he also liked walking along what he called 'the road to Tarascon'. His painting, of which this is a quick sketch, combines these two themes.*

. . . Have you reread *Tartarin* yet? Be sure not to forget. Do you remember that wonderful page in *Tartarin*, the complaint of the old Tarascon diligence? Well, I have just painted that red and green vehicle in the courtyard of the inn. You will see it. This hasty sketch gives you the composition, a simple foreground of grey gravel, a very, very simple background too, pink and yellow walls, with windows with green shutters, and a patch of blue sky [80]. The two carriages very brightly coloured, green and red, the wheels—yellow, black, blue and orange. Again a size 30 canvas. The carriages are painted like a Monticelli [French painter who died in 1886] with spots of thickly laid-on paint. . .

Now imagine an immense pine tree of greenish-blue, spreading its branches horizontally over a bright green lawn, and gravel splashed with light and shade. Two figures of lovers in the shade of the great tree: size 30 canvas. This very simple patch of garden is brightened by beds of geraniums, orange in the distance under the black branches [82].

Then two more size 30 canvases, the Trinquetaille bridge and another bridge, along the road where the railway is. . . The Trinquetaille bridge with all these steps is a canvas done on a grey morning, the stones, the asphalt, the pavements are grey; the sky, pale blue; the figures, coloured; and there is a sickly tree with yellow foliage [83]. . .

[552] Ever yours, Vincent

82 Public garden with a couple and a blue fir tree
Opposite: Vincent probably put this painting in Gauguin's bedroom, which overlooked the small park. He sent the sketch (above [81]) to Theo.

83 The Trinquetaille bridge
Opposite: This was the only road bridge across the Rhône at Arles, crossing to the suburb of Trinquetaille. Vincent's unusual perspective is from the road running along the river bank, looking up the steps to the bridge.

84 The viaduct and The Trinquetaille bridge
Sketches of two of Vincent's paintings from Arles. The larger sketch shows the two railway viaducts that lay just behind the Yellow House in the avenue de Montmajour.

To Gauguin, 17 October 1888

My dear Gauguin,

Thanks for your letter, and above all thanks for your promise to come here as early as the twentieth. . .

Listen, the other day I wrote you that my eyesight was strangely tired. All right, I rested for two and a half days, and then I set to work again, but without daring to go out into the open air yet. I have done, still for my decoration, a size 30 canvas of my bedroom with the white deal furniture that you know [71]. Well, I enormously enjoyed doing this interior of nothing at all, of a Seurat-like simplicity; with flat tints, but brushed on roughly, with a thick impasto, the walls pale lilac, the ground a faded broken red, the chair and the bed chrome yellow, the pillows and the sheet a very pale green-citron, the counterpane blood red, the washstand orange, the washbasin blue, the window green. By means of all these very diverse tones I have wanted to express an *absolute restfulness*, you see, and there is no white in it at all except the little note produced by the mirror with its black frame (in order to get the fourth pair of complementaries into it).

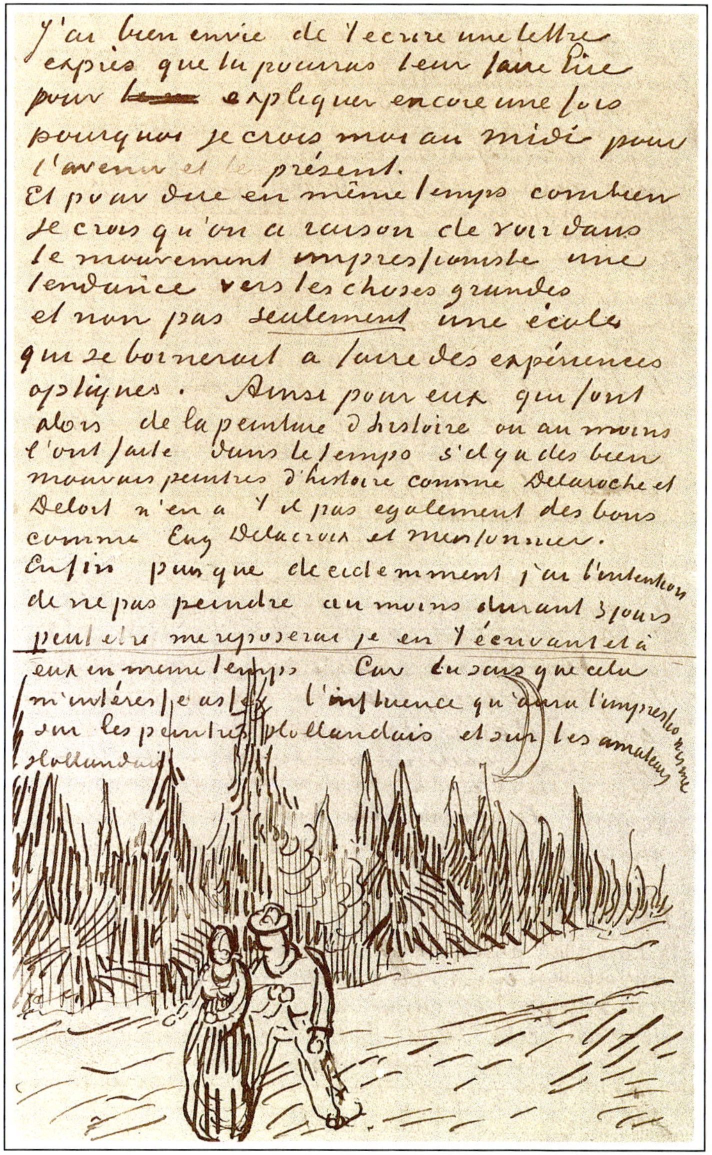

J'ai bien envie de t'écrire une lettre
exprès que tu pourras leur faire lire
pour expliquer encore une fois
pourquoi je crois moi au midi pour
l'avenir et le présent.
Et pour dire en même temps combien
je crois qu'on a raison de voir dans
le mouvement impressioniste une
tendance vers les choses grandes
et non pas seulement une école
qui se bornerait à faire des expériences
optiques. Ainsi pour eux qui font
alors de la peinture d'histoire ou au moins
l'ont faite dans le temps s'il y a des bien
mauvais peintres d'histoire comme Delaroche et
Delort n'en a t il pas également des bons
comme Eug Delacroix et Meissonnier.
Enfin puisque décidemment j'ai l'intention
de ne pas peindre au moins durant 3 jours
peut être me reposerai je en t'écrivant et à
eux en même temps. Car tu sais que cela
m'intéresse assez l'influence qu'aura l'impressionisme
sur les peintres hollandais et sur les amateurs
hollandais

85 A LANE OF CYPRESSES WITH A COUPLE WALKING
Vincent sketched his painting of the flame-like trees that were to dominate so many of his later pictures at Saint-Rémy.

Well, you will see it along with the other things, and we will talk about it, for I often don't know what I am doing when I am working almost like a sleep-walker.

It is beginning to turn cold, particularly on the days when the mistral blows.

I have had gas laid on in the studio, so that we shall have good light in winter.

Perhaps Arles will disappoint you, if you come here in mistral weather; but you wait. . . It is only in the long run that the poetry of this place penetrates.

You will not find the house as comfortable yet as we shall gradually try to make it. There are so many expenses! And it can't be done all at once. But I believe after all that once you are here you will be seized like me with a rage for painting the autumnal effects in the intervals between the spells of mistral, and that you will understand why I insisted on your coming here, now that we are having very fine weather.

Well, we'll see each other.

[B22] Ever yours, Vincent

To Theo, c.21 October 1888

MY DEAR THEO,

. . .Here is a very rough sketch of my last canvas, a row of green cypresses against a pink sky with a crescent moon in pale citron. An indefinite foreground, sand and some thistles. Two lovers, the man in pale blue with a yellow hat, the woman with a pink bodice and a black skirt [85]. That makes the fourth canvas of 'The Poet's Garden,' which is the scheme of decoration for Gauguin's room. . .

[556] Ever yours, Vincent

Gauguin

86 VINCENT'S CHAIR
This image was based on the illustration by the English artist Luke Fildes of the 'empty chair' of Dickens after the novelist's death. Vincent's own interpretation includes his pipe and tobacco pouch.

Gauguin finally arrived in Arles on 23 October 1888. Vincent was full of hopes; Gauguin was his mentor, an experienced painter who would provide support and encouragement.

Gauguin's own expectations were very different. He had delayed coming to Arles for months, partly because he realized that Vincent would not be an easy companion. Eventually Theo proposed a deal that he decided to accept: the art dealer would pay him 150 francs a month, in return for one painting. As soon as Gauguin arrived he wondered whether he was mistaken to come. He could see that Vincent lived a chaotic life and was unable to cope with everyday tasks. He also feared that Vincent's elated mood and high expectations would lead to problems.

Gauguin was an equally difficult companion, a man with strong opinions who found it difficult to compromise. From the start the two men argued. They tried to paint the same subjects, but the differences between their approaches soon became a source of tension. Gauguin would tell Vincent that he should work from his imagination, whereas Vincent was striving to capture the essence of what he saw in front of him. These arguments became increasingly heated, culminating in a row after a visit to the Musée Fabre at Montpellier in December.

They returned to Arles exhausted, the air full of tensions that had come to the surface. Gauguin felt so frustrated that he wrote to Theo, saying that he was returning to Paris. Vincent, terrified at the prospect of losing his companion, pleaded for his friend to stay. Gauguin relented and dropped his plan to leave.

87 GAUGUIN'S CHAIR
The 'companion' to 'Vincent's Chair' [86], portraying the much more comfortable chair of his friend. It was painted just a month before the incident that led to Gauguin's departure.

88 Sower and Trunk of an old yew tree
These sketches show two of the paintings that were among the first Vincent did after Gauguin's arrival.

To Theo, 24 October 1888

My dear Theo,

Thanks for your letter and the 50-fr. note. As you learned from my wire, Gauguin has arrived in good health. He even seems to me better than I am.

Of course he is very pleased with the sale you have effected [Theo had just sold a painting by Gauguin], and I no less. . . Gauguin will certainly write to you today. He is very interesting as a man. . . He will probably produce a great deal here, and I hope perhaps I shall too.

And then I dare hope that the burden will be a *little* less heavy for you, and I even hope, *much* less heavy. I myself realize the necessity of producing even to the extent of being mentally crushed and physically drained by it, just because after all I have no other means of ever getting back what we have spent.

I cannot help it that my pictures do not sell.

Nevertheless the time will come when people will see that they are worth more than the price of the paint . . .

[557] Ever yours, Vincent

To Theo, 28 October 1888

My dear Theo,

. . .This week I made a new study of a sower, the landscape quite flat, the figure small and vague.

Further I have made another study of a ploughed field with the stump of an old yew tree. Like this [88]. . .

What Gauguin tells of the Tropics seems marvellous to me. Surely the future of a great renaissance in painting lies there. . .

89 Trunk of an old yew tree
Vincent's unusual view shows the lower part of the tree dominating the ploughed field.

I regret I am not ten or twenty years younger, then I would certainly go there.

Now it is most unlikely that I shall leave the shore to put to sea, and the little Yellow House here in Arles will remain a way station between Africa, the Tropics, and the people of the North. . .

[558b] Ever yours, Vincent

To Bernard, c.2 November 1888

MY DEAR COMRADE BERNARD,

. . . For a long time now it has seemed to me that in our nasty profession of painting we are most sorely in need of men with the hands and the stomachs of workmen. More natural tastes—more loving and more charitable temperaments—than the decadent dandies of the Parisian boulevards have.

Well, here we are without the slightest doubt in the presence of a virgin creature with savage instincts. With Gauguin blood and sex prevail over ambition.

But enough, you have seen him at close range for a longer time than I have; I only wanted to tell you in a few words what my first impressions are. . . Gauguin is working on a canvas of the same night café I painted too [68], but with figures seen in the brothels. It promises to turn out beautiful.

I myself have done two studies of the fall of leaves in an avenue of poplars [90], and a third study of this whole avenue. . .

[B19a] Sincerely yours, Vincent

90 THE ALYSCAMPS, AVENUE AT ARLES
This was the town's ancient burial ground, dating from the third century AD. *Vincent painted the view looking down on the stone tombs from the adjacent bank of the Canal de Craponne.*

91 L'ARLÉSIENNE (MADAME GINOUX), WITH GLOVES AND PARASOL
Marie Ginoux and her husband ran the Café de la Gare, where Vincent had stayed until he moved into the Yellow House.

To Theo, c.6 November 1888

MY DEAR THEO,

. . . I have an Arlésienne at last, a figure (size 30 canvas) slashed on in an hour, background pale citron, the face grey, the clothes black, black, black, with perfectly raw Prussian blue. She is leaning on a green table and seated in an armchair of orange wood [91].

Gauguin has bought a chest of drawers for the house, and various household utensils, and also 20 metres of very strong canvas, a lot of things that we needed. . .

I think you will like the falling leaves that I have done.

It is some poplar trunks in lilac cut by the frame where the leaves begin.

92 THE RED VINEYARD
Tradition has it that this was the only painting that Vincent sold in his lifetime. The picture was bought by Anna Boch, sister of the Belgian artist Eugène.

These tree trunks are lined like pillars along an avenue where there are rows of old Roman tombs of a blue lilac right and left. And then the soil is covered with a thick carpet of yellow and orange fallen leaves. And they are still falling like flakes of snow.

And in the avenue, little black figures of lovers. . .

But on Sunday if you had been with us, you would have seen a red vineyard, all red like red wine. In the distance it turned to yellow, and then a green sky with the sun, the earth after the rain violet, sparkling yellow here and there where it caught the reflection of the setting sun [92]. . .

[559] Ever yours, Vincent

To Wil, c.16 November 1888

MY DEAR SISTER,

. . . I have just finished painting, to put in my bedroom, a memory of the garden at Etten; here is a scratch of it. It is rather a large canvas. Here are the details of the colours. The younger of the two ladies who are out for a walk is wearing a Scottish shawl with green and orange checks, and a red parasol. The old lady has a violet shawl, nearly black [93]. . .

93 MEMORY OF THE GARDEN AT ETTEN
A painting from Vincent's imagination, inspired by Gauguin's example. At the same time Gauguin was working on a similar picture based on the 'poet's garden', the 'Garden at Arles'.

Let us suppose that the two ladies out for a walk are you and our mother; let us even suppose that there is not the least, absolutely not the least vulgar and fatuous resemblance—yet the deliberate choice of the colour, the sombre violet with the blotch of violent citron yellow of the dahlias, suggests Mother's personality to me.

94 *SKETCH OF* MEMORY OF THE GARDEN AT ETTEN
Vincent made the sketch for his sister Wil, the younger woman depicted on the far left of the picture.

The figure in the Scotch plaid with orange and green checks stands out against the sombre green of the cypress, which contrast is further accentuated by the red parasol—this figure gives me an impression of you like those in Dickens's novels, a vaguely representative figure.

I don't know whether you can understand that one may make a poem only by arranging colours, in the same way that one can say comforting things in music. . .

In a similar manner the bizarre lines, purposely selected and multiplied, meandering all through the picture, may fail to give the

garden a vulgar resemblance, but may present it to our minds as seen in a dream, depicting its character, and at the same time stranger than it is in reality.

I have also painted 'A Woman Reading a Novel' [95], the luxuriant hair very black, a green bodice, the sleeves the colour of wine lees, the skirt black, the background all yellow, bookshelves with books. She is holding a yellow book in her hands.

So much for today. But I remember I have not told you that my friend Paul Gauguin, an Impressionist painter, is now living with me, and that we are very happy together. He strongly encourages me to work often from pure imagination.

Give my kindest regards to Mother, and do not fail to send me Mrs. Mauve's address by return mail.

I embrace you in thought, Mother and you.

[W9] Yours, Vincent

95 WOMAN READING A NOVEL
A sketch of a painting. Vincent, an avid reader, frequently included books in his pictures.

96 SOWER WITH SETTING SUN
This sketch of Vincent's last 'sower' painting of the season was influenced both by Gauguin's 'Vision After the Sermon' and by the Japanese prints that they both admired.

To Theo, c.25 November 1888

MY DEAR THEO,

. . . This is a sketch of the latest canvas I am working on, another 'Sower' [96]. An immense citron-yellow disc for the sun. A green-yellow sky with pink clouds. The field violet, the sower and the tree Prussian blue. . .

Here the weather is cold, notwithstanding which one sees very fine things. For instance yesterday evening an extraordinarily beautiful sunset of a mysterious, sickly citron colour—Prussian blue cypresses against trees with dead leaves in all sorts of broken tones without any speckling with bright greens.

You cannot imagine how much it pleases me that you have painters staying with you, and that you are not living all alone in

your apartment, just as it pleases me very much to have such good company as Gauguin's.

I shall write again soon, and once more thanks for your kind letter.

[558a] Ever yours, Vincent

97 JOSEPH ROULIN, HEAD
Vincent had become friends with the postman Roulin in the summer and he painted portraits of every member of the family.

To Theo, c.4 December 1888

MY DEAR THEO,

. . . I have made portraits *of a whole family*, that of the postman whose head I had done previously—the man, his wife, the baby, the little boy, and the son of sixteen, all characters and very French, though the first has the look of a Russian. Size 15 canvases. You know how I feel about this. . . If I manage to do this *whole family* better still, at least I shall have done something to my liking and something individual. Just now I am completely swamped with studies, studies, studies, and this will go on for quite a while—it makes such a mess that it breaks my heart, and yet it will provide me with some property when I'm forty. . .

[560] Vincent

98 PORTRAIT OF CAMILLE ROULIN
Camille was an eleven-year-old schoolboy.

To Theo, mid-December 1888

MY DEAR THEO,

Yesterday Gauguin and I went to Montpellier to see the gallery. . .

Gauguin and I talked a lot about Delacroix, Rembrandt, etc. Our arguments are terribly *electric*, sometimes we come out of them with our heads as exhausted as a used electric battery . . .

[564] Ever yours, Vincent

To Theo, 23 December 1888

My dear Theo,

Thank you very much for your letter, for the 100-fr. note enclosed and also for the 50-fr. money order.

I think myself that Gauguin was a little out of sorts with the good town of Arles, the little Yellow House where we work, and especially with me.

As a matter of fact, there are bound to be grave difficulties to overcome here too, for him as well as for me.

But these difficulties are more within ourselves than outside.

Altogether I think that either he will definitely go, or else definitely stay.

I told him to think it over and make his calculations all over again before doing anything.

Gauguin is very powerful, strongly creative, but just because of that he must have peace.

Will he find it anywhere if he does not find it here?

I am waiting for him to make a decision with absolute serenity.

A good handshake.

[565] Vincent

99 Portrait of Armand Roulin
Seventeen-year-old Armand was an apprentice blacksmith.

100 Augustine Roulin with Baby
Madame Roulin later served as the model for Vincent's 'La Berceuse' [104]. Marcelle was four months old when she was painted.

101 SELF-PORTRAIT WITH BANDAGED EAR
This was painted just a few days after Vincent had cut off the lobe of his ear. In the background is his easel and one of his favourite Japanese prints by Sato Torakiyo.

The Crisis

102 PLATE WITH ONIONS, 'ANNUAIRE DE LA SANTÉ', AND OTHER OBJECTS
The book on the table is one advocating natural therapy. Beside it are Vincent's pipe and a letter he had just received from Theo. This work, completed a few days after Vincent left hospital, was proof that his artistic ability had not been affected by the mental breakdown.

On the evening of 23 December 1888 when Gauguin was walking among the oleanders in the public garden, he heard footsteps and, turning around, he was astonished to see Vincent giving him a threatening look. Gauguin stared back and Vincent retreated into the Yellow House.

Gauguin spent the night in a hotel, and returned to the Yellow House the following morning to find Vincent lying on his bed, bleeding profusely. The story, which emerged later, was that he had sliced off part of his ear lobe, taking it to a local prostitute called Rachel. A doctor was summoned and Vincent was later sent to hospital. Theo was informed and, fearing that his brother might be close to death, he immediately came to see him in Arles.

Fortunately Vincent's condition improved and, after spending Christmas Day in Arles, Theo and Gauguin returned to Paris the following day. After a week of severe depression, Vincent's mental and physical health improved and by New Year's Eve he was regaining his strength and was ready to start thinking of painting again. On 7 January 1889 he returned to the Yellow House.

Just before Christmas Theo had become engaged to Jo Bonger, the sister of his friend Andries. Theo had planned to return to Holland to break the news to his mother over the holidays, but his brother's mental breakdown intervened. Vincent felt ambivalent about Theo's engagement. Although he wanted Theo to find happiness, he was only too aware that the arrival of a bride might rob him of the emotional and financial support that he received from his brother.

To Theo, 2 January 1889

MY DEAR THEO,

So as to reassure you completely on my account, I write you these few lines in the office of M. Rey, the house surgeon, whom you met yourself. I shall stay here at the hospital a few days more, then I think I can count on returning to the house very quietly.

Now I beg only one thing of you, not to worry, because that would cause me one worry *too many*.

Now let's talk about our friend Gauguin. Have I scared him? In short, why doesn't he give me any sign of life? He must have left with you. Besides, it was necessary for him to go back to Paris, and he will perhaps feel more at home in Paris than here. Tell Gauguin to write to me, and that I am always thinking about him. . .

[567] Ever yours, Vincent

103 DR FÉLIX REY, BUST

Curiously, the doctor who treated Vincent's mutilated ear has himself been shown with a bright red ear. Dr Rey, who was given the picture, disliked it and used it to block up a hole in his chicken house.

To Theo, 4 January 1889

MY DEAR BOY,

I hope that Gauguin will reassure you completely, and also a little about the painting business.

I expect to start work again soon.

The charwoman and my friend Roulin have taken care of the house, and have put everything in order. . .

My dear boy, I am so terribly distressed over your journey. I should have wished you had been spared that, for after all no harm came to me, and there was no reason why you should be so upset.

I cannot tell you how glad I am that you have made peace, and even more than that, with the Bongers [Theo had just announced his engagement to Jo Bonger, sister of his friend Andries].

Tell this to Andries for me, and give him my cordial regards. What would I not have given for you to have seen Arles when it was fine; now you have seen it in mourning.

[566] Ever yours, Vincent

Write a line to Mother for me too, so that no one will be worried.

To Gauguin, 4 January 1889

MY DEAR FRIEND GAUGUIN,

I take the opportunity of my first absence from the hospital to write you a few words of very deep and sincere friendship. I often thought of you in the hospital, even at the height of fever and comparative weakness.

Look here—was my brother Theo's journey really necessary?. . .

Now at least to reassure him completely, and I entreat you, be confident yourself that after all no evil exists in this best of worlds in which everything is for the best.

Then I should like you to give my kind regards to good old Schuffenecker [an artist friend], to refrain, until after more mature reflection on both our parts, from speaking ill of our poor little Yellow House, and to remember me to the painters whom I saw in Paris. I wish you prosperity in Paris, with a good handshake.

[566] Yours sincerely, Vincent

To Theo, 9 January 1889

MY DEAR THEO,

Even before receiving (this very moment) your kind letter, I had had a letter this morning from your fiancée announcing the

engagement. So I have already sent her my sincere congratulations in reply, and herewith I repeat them to you. . .

This morning I was again at the hospital to get another dressing, and I walked for an hour and a half with the house surgeon [Dr Rey], and we talked a bit about everything, even about natural history. . .

Physically I am well, the wound is healing very well and the great loss of blood is being made up, because I eat and digest well. What is *to be feared* most is insomnia, and the doctor has not spoken about it to me, nor have I spoken of it to him either. . .

I fight this insomnia by a very, very strong dose of camphor in my pillow and mattress and, if ever you can't sleep, I recommend this to you. I was very much afraid of sleeping alone in the house, and I have been afraid I should not be able to sleep. . .

With a handshake, and of course you know how I wish you happy days with your fiancée.

[570] Ever yours, Vincent

To Theo, 17 January 1889

MY DEAR THEO,

. . .I have started work again, and I already have three finished studies in the studio, besides the portrait of Dr Rey, which I gave him as a keepsake [103]. So there is no worse harm done this time than a little more suffering and its attendant wretchedness. And I keep on hoping. But I feel weak and rather uneasy and frightened. . .

Rey told me that being very impressionable was enough to account for the attack that I had, and that I was really only anæmic, but that I really must feed myself up. . .

[571] Yours, Vincent

To Gauguin, c.22 January 1889

MY DEAR FRIEND GAUGUIN,

Thanks for your letter. Remaining alone on board my little Yellow House—though perhaps it was my duty to be the last to stay—I was really quite pissed off by the departure of my friends.

Roulin [the postman] has had his transfer to Marseilles and has just left. It was touching to see him these last days with little Marcelle when he made her laugh and bounced her on his knees.

His transfer has meant separation from his family and that he, whom simultaneously one evening you and I nicknamed 'the passer-by', should be very heavy-hearted won't surprise you. I too bear witness to that and other heart-breaking things. When he sang to his child his voice took on a strange timbre mingling the voice of a lullaby or a sad nursemaid and then another brazen note like a French clarion.

At the present time I'm very sorry that I insisted so much that you should stay here and wait for events and gave you so many good reasons for that at the present time I'm very sorry that I may have brought about your departure—unless that departure had been previously determinéd?

And then it was perhaps up to me to show that I still had the right to be kept frankly in the picture.

Have you read and re-read Beecher Stowe's *Uncle Tom's Cabin.* It's perhaps not very well written from the literary point of view. Have you already read *Germinie Lacerteux* [a novel by the brothers Goncourt published in 1864].

Whatever happens I hope we have enough affection for each other to be able to start again if necessary if being broke—alas always the situation for us artists without capital—requires it.

You mention in your letter one of my canvases 'The Sunflowers' on a yellow background—meaning that you would

This letter, published here for the first time in English, was sent just a month after Gauguin's sudden departure. Vincent jumps from one subject to another—from the question of returning Gauguin's possessions to a description of his latest painting, and its disjointed style and obscure references reveal Vincent's disturbed state of mind. In the aftermath of his breakdown, Vincent displays ambivalent feelings towards his old friend.

like to have it [64]. I don't think you are far out in your choice—if Jeannin [a French painter] has the peony and Quost [another painter, whose flower pictures, together with those of Jeannin, Vincent greatly admired] the hollyhocks I myself would have taken the sunflower [*sic*].

I think I shall begin by sending back what belongs to you and asking you to note that it is my intention after what happened to contest categorically your right to the canvas in question. But as I approve your intelligence in the choice of this canvas I will make an effort to paint two more exactly alike. In that case it could definitely be arranged in a friendly manner that you could still have yours. Yesterday I started work again on the canvas I had painted of Madame Roulin ['La Berceuse'], the one, in which because of my accident the hands had been left vague [104]. As an arrangement of colours the reds shading into pure oranges increasing again in the flesh tones graduating into chrome passing through pinks combining with olive and Veronese greens. As an arrangement of Impressionist colours I've never done anything better.

104 AUGUSTINE ROULIN OR LA BERCEUSE
Vincent painted the postman's wife pulling the string that rocked her baby Marcelle's cradle. This was one of his favourite pictures and he later painted five copies of it.

And I think that if you put this picture just as it is on a fishing boat even one belonging to Icelanders there would be some among them who would feel it to be a cradle song. Ah! my dear friend painting is to us what the music of Berlioz and Wagner was before us—a consolatory art for sore hearts! And yet there are only a few like you and me who feel it!!!

My brother understands you and when he tells me you're another unhappy wretch like me that proves he understands us. I'll send on your belongings but at times my weakness returns and then I can't even go through the motions of sending on your belongings. In a few days I'll be strong again. And the 'masks and mailed gloves' (use as little as possible less childish war engines) these terrible instruments of war [which Gauguin had left in the

Yellow House] will have to wait until then. I'm writing to you very calmly but the packing up of all the rest I haven't been able to do. During my brain fever, nervous breakdown or attack of madness—I don't know how to explain or describe it, my mind sailed over a great many oceans. I dreamt of the Dutchman's phantom ship as well as the Horla [an evil Spirit in a short story by de Maupassant] and it seems I sang though at other times I don't know how to sing except an old lullaby remembering the song the nursemaid sang that rocked the sailors that I was trying to create in an arrangement of colours [a reference to 'La Berceuse'] before I became ill. Fit[*sic*].

Not knowing the music of Berlioz.

Handshake with all my heart.

Entirely yours, Vincent

It would please me if you could write to me again soon.

Have you read the complete Tartarin now southern imagination makes everyone pals and between us we always have friendship.

To Theo, 22 January 1889

MY DEAR THEO,

. . .I am working on the portrait of Roulin's wife, which I was working on before I was ill [104].

In it I have ranged the reds from pink to an orange which rises up from the yellows to citron, with light and sombre greens. If I could finish it, I should be very glad, but I am afraid she will not want to pose with her husband away.

You can see just what a disaster Gauguin's leaving is, because it has pushed us down again just when we had made a home. . .

[573]

Ever yours, Vincent

To Koning, c.23 January 1889

My dear friend Koning,

Thanks for having wished me a happy New Year all the way from the North of our native country. I received your postcard in the hospital at Arles, where I had been quartered following an attack of something the matter with my brains, or otherwise fever, which had nearly passed off already. . .

At present I have in mind, or rather on my easel, the portrait of a woman. I call it 'La Berceuse' [104]. . . It is a woman in a green dress (the bust olive green and the skirt pale malachite green).

The hair is quite orange and in plaits. The complexion is chrome yellow, worked up with some naturally broken tones for the purpose of modelling.

The hands holding the rope of the cradle, the same.

At the bottom the background is vermilion (simply representing a tiled floor or else a stone floor). The wall is covered with wallpaper, which of course I have calculated in conformity with the rest of the colours. This wallpaper is bluish-green with pink dahlias spotted with orange and ultramarine. . .

[571a] Your friend, Vincent

To Theo, 28 January 1889

My dear Theo,

Only a few words to tell you that my health and my work are not progressing so badly.

It astonishes me already when I compare my condition today with what it was a month ago. Before that I knew well enough that one could fracture one's legs and arms and recover afterward,

but I did not know that you could fracture the brain in your head and recover from that too. . .

[574] Ever yours, Vincent

To Theo, 3 February 1889

MY DEAR THEO,

. . .I must tell you this, that the neighbours, etc., are particularly kind to me, as everyone here is suffering either from fever, or hallucinations, or madness, we understand each other like members of the same family. Yesterday I went to see the girl [the prostitute Rachel] I had gone to when I was out of my wits. They told me there that in this country things like that are not out of the ordinary. She had been upset by it and had fainted but had recovered her calm. And they spoke well of her, too.

But as for considering myself as completely sane, we must not do it. People here who have been ill like me have told me the truth. You may be old or young, but there will always be moments when you lose your head. . . So I do not ask you to say of me that there is nothing wrong with me, or that there never will be.

[576] Ever yours, Vincent

To Theo, c.17 February 1889

MY DEAR THEO,

I have been so completely out of sorts mentally that it would have been useless to try to write an answer to your kind letter. Today I have just come home provisionally, I hope for good. . .

[577] Ever yours, Vincent

Relapse

When Vincent returned to the Yellow House he hoped that he was cured. His mutilated ear was healing and he was set on resuming his painting as soon as possible. But by early February 1889 he was suffering from another mental breakdown again, obsessed with paranoid fears that he was being poisoned. On 7 February he was taken back to hospital, where he was kept for ten days.

When Vincent returned again to the Yellow House, his neighbours in the place Lamartine were concerned about his presence and presented a petition to the mayor asking for him to be removed. On 25 February the police came to escort him back to the hospital cell and the Yellow House was officially closed. Vincent's condition improved in hospital and at the end of March he was allowed out for short spells in order to paint. By this time, however, the terrible truth was dawning upon him: he seemed to be subject to recurring mental breakdowns. He realized that it would be difficult for him to look after himself and it might be necessary to find an institution to care for him.

At the time when Vincent was about to retreat from the world his brother Theo was embarking on a new life. He had become engaged to Jo Bonger at Christmas and on 17 April they married. Vincent feared that he would lose some of Theo's affection to the new bride. These fears were groundless, but they may well have been in Vincent's mind when he made the difficult decision to enter a mental asylum.

106 THE COURTYARD OF THE HOSPITAL
Vincent drew the view from the first floor, looking down on to the elegant central courtyard.

105 DORMITORY IN THE HOSPITAL
Opposite: The patients are huddled around a stove in the long dormitory of the sixteenth-century hospital in Arles.

107 VINCENT'S LETTER
Writing from his hospital bed, following his second mental breakdown, Vincent was short of paper and wrote on the envelope of Theo's letter.

To Theo, 19 March 1889

MY DEAR BROTHER,

. . . Here I am, shut up in a cell all the livelong day, under lock and key and with keepers, without my guilt being proved or even open to proof.

Needless to say, in the secret tribunal of my soul I have much to reply to all that. Needless to say, I cannot be angry, and it seems to me a case of *qui s'excuse s'accuse.* Only to let you know that as for setting me free—mind, I do not ask it, being persuaded that the whole accusation will be reduced to nothing—but I do say that as for getting me freed, you would find it difficult. If I did not restrain my indignation, I should at once be thought a dangerous lunatic. Let us hope and have patience. Besides, strong emotion can only aggravate my case. That is why I beg you for the present to let things be. . .

[579] Ever yours, Vincent

To Signac, c.10 April 1889

MY DEAR FRIEND SIGNAC,

. . . I remain greatly obliged to you for your friendly and beneficial visit, which contributed considerably to raising of my spirits Paul Signac visited Vincent on 23–4 March on his way from Paris to Cassis]. At present I am well, and I work at the sanatorium and its environs. I have just come back with two studies of orchards. . .

The big one is a poor landscape with little cottages. . . The other landscape is nearly all green with a little lilac and grey. . .

[583b] Yours sincerely, Vincent

108 *SKETCH OF* THE CRAU WITH PEACH TREES IN BLOOM
Vincent sketched the painting of peach blossoms for his artist friend Signac.

To Theo, c.21 April 1889

MY DEAR THEO,

. . . I feel quite unable to take a new studio and to stay there alone—here in Arles or elsewhere, for the moment it is all the same; I have tried to make up my mind to begin again, but at the moment it's not possible.

I should be afraid of losing the power to work, which is coming back to me now, by forcing myself and by having all the other responsibilities of a studio on my shoulders besides.

And temporarily I wish to remain shut up as much for my own peace of mind as for other people's. . .

109 THE CRAU WITH PEACH TREES IN BLOOM
At the end of March Vincent was able to go out into the countryside and paint. This landscape, done from the same place as 'Harvest Landscape' [49], showed that he had lost none of his abilities. The blossom must have reminded him of his arrival in Arles the year before.

These last days were sad, with all the moving, taking away all my furniture, packing up the canvases that are going to you, but the thing I felt saddest about was that you had given me all these things with such brotherly love, and that for so many years you were always the one who supported me, and then to be obliged to come back and tell you this sorry tale—but it's difficult to express it as I felt it. . .

All your kindness to me seemed greater than ever to me today. I can't put the way I feel it in words, but I assure you that this kindness had been pure gold, and if you do not see any results from it, my dear brother, don't fret about it; your own goodness abides. Only transfer this affection to your wife as much as possible. And if we correspond somewhat less, you will see that if she is what I think her, she will comfort you. That is what I hope. . .

[585] Ever yours, Vincent

To Wil, 30 April 1889

My dear sister,

. . .I am going to an asylum in Saint-Rémy, not far from here, for three months. I have had in all four great crises, during which I didn't in the least know what I said, what I wanted and what I did. Not taking into account that I had previously had three fainting fits without any plausible reason, and without retaining the slightest remembrance of what I felt.

Well, this is bad enough, though the fact is that I have been much calmer since then, and that I am perfectly well physically. I still feel incapable of taking a new studio. Notwithstanding this I am working, and I have just finished two pictures of the hospital, one of a ward, a very long ward, with rows of beds with white curtains, in which some figures of patients are moving [105]. The

110 THE COURTYARD OF THE HOSPITAL
Vincent continued to visit the hospital as an outpatient, developing a friendship with Dr Rey, the physician who treated him. He painted this view when the spring flowers had come out.

walls, the ceiling with big beams, all in white, lilac-white or green-white. . . And then, as a pendant, the inner court. It is an arcaded gallery like those one finds in Arab buildings, all whitewashed. In front of those galleries an antique garden with a pond in the middle, and eight flower beds, forget-me-nots, Christmas roses, anemones, ranunculus, wallflowers, daisies, and so on. And under the gallery orange trees and oleander. So it is a picture quite full of flowers and vernal green. However, three gloomy black tree trunks pass through it like serpents, and in the foreground four big dismal clusters of sombre box shrub [110]. . .

I am unable to describe exactly what is the matter with me; now and then there are horrible fits of anxiety, apparently without cause, or otherwise a feeling of emptiness and fatigue in the head. . .

[W11] All yours, Vincent

· Saint-Rémy ·

Vincent needed a retreat where he would be cared for, yet continue to paint. Reluctantly he decided to go to a mental asylum in Saint-Rémy, a small town nestling under the hills of the Alpilles.

111 Road menders in a lane with heavy plane trees
Opposite: The medieval centre of Saint-Rémy was surrounded by ramparts and an elegant circular road. Vincent's view shows the boulevard Mirabeau, looking south.

112 Bird's-eye view of the village
This view is similar to the one that Vincent would have seen when walking down the hill from the asylum into Saint-Rémy.

113 WINDOW OF VINCENT'S STUDIO AT THE ASYLUM
As well as his bedroom cell, Vincent was given another room to use as his studio. The two paintings hanging on the wall on the right are studies of trees, possibly those visible through the barred window.

To the Asylum

114 THE VESTIBULE OF THE ASYLUM
The doorway looks out to the fountain. Lying just inside is a framed picture, probably one of Vincent's paintings of the garden outside.

On 8 May Vincent travelled to Saint-Rémy-de-Provence, fifteen miles north east of Arles, accompanied by his friend the Reverend Frédéric Salles, pastor of the Reformed Protestant Church. The asylum of Saint-Paul-de-Mausole, half a mile to the south of the small town, was set beside what had once been an Augustinian monastery. As he entered its gates, Vincent must have thought how his high hopes of the previous year had been dashed: instead of setting up a 'studio of the South' he was entering institution for the mentally ill.

On his arrival, Dr Théophile Peyron wrote in the asylum's medical register that his new patient was 'suffering from acute mania with hallucinations of sight and hearing which have caused him to mutilate himself by cutting off his right ear. . . It is my opinion that M. van Gogh is subject to epileptic fits at very infrequent intervals.' For Vincent, who was lucid for most of the time, it must have been an act of desperation to have to enter a mental asylum, where the majority of the patients were insane. He can have had nothing in common with most of his fellow inmates. But despite his apparent calmness, Vincent realized that he now had an increased vulnerability to surprise attacks during which he would fall into a deep depression. When he was gripped by one of these paranoid moods, he wanted to end his life.

115 A PASSAGEWAY AT THE ASYLUM
The cell that Vincent was given to use as a studio may well have been the one that the figure is entering.

To Theo, c.10–15 May 1889

116 IRISES
This was the first picture that Vincent did at Saint-Rémy; it was painted in the garden of the asylum.

MY DEAR THEO,

Thanks for your letter. You are quite right to say that M. Salles has been splendid all through. I am under a great obligation to him.

I wanted to tell you that I think I have done well to come here; first of all, by seeing the *reality* of the life of the various madmen and lunatics in this menagerie, I am losing the vague dread, the fear of the thing. And little by little I can come to look upon madness as a disease like any other. Then the change of surroundings does me good, I think.

As far as I can make out, the doctor here is inclined to consider that I have had some sort of epileptic attack. But I did not ask him about it.

Have you received the case of pictures? I am anxious to know whether or not they have suffered.

I am working on two others—some violet irises [116] and a lilac bush, two subjects taken from the garden.

The idea of work as a duty is coming back to me very strongly, and I think that all my faculties for work will come back to me fairly quickly. Only work often absorbs me so much that I think I shall always remain absent-minded and awkward in shifting for myself for the rest of my life too.

I shall not write you a long letter—I will try to reply to my new sister's [Theo's wife Jo] letter, which touched me very much, but I do not know if I shall manage to do it.

A handshake.

[591] Ever yours, Vincent

117 BARRED WINDOWS
This was probably the window of Vincent's bedroom cell. From here he overlooked the wheatfield that he drew and painted so often.

118 Sunflower triptych
Vincent told Theo that he wanted two of his sunflower paintings displayed as wings to the picture of the postman's wife, Madame Roulin, 'La Berceuse'.

To sister-in-law Jo, c.10–15 May 1889

My dear sister,

. . . Though here there are some patients very seriously ill, the fear and horror of madness that I used to have has already lessened a great deal. And though here you continually hear terrible cries and howls like beasts in a menagerie, in spite of that people get to know each other very well and help each other when their attacks come on. When I am working in the garden, they all come to look, and I assure you they have the discretion and manners to leave me alone—more than the good people of the town of Arles, for instance. . .

[591] Your brother, Vincent

119 Trees with ivy
Vincent painted in the garden in front of his studio cell. Redolent with symbolism, ivy had always been among his favourite plants.

To Theo, 22 May 1889

My dear Theo,

. . .If you arrange them [my pictures] this way, say 'La Berceuse' in the middle and the two canvases of 'Sunflowers' to the right and left, it makes a sort of triptych [118].

And then the yellow and orange tones of the head will gain in brilliance by the proximity of the yellow wings.

And then you will understand what I wrote to you, that my idea had been to make a sort of decoration . . .

Here is a new size 30 canvas . . . which represents the eternal nests of greenery for lovers [119].

Some thick tree trunks covered with ivy, the ground also covered with ivy and periwinkle, a stone bench and a bush of pale

roses in the cold shadow. In the foreground some plants with white calyxes. It is green, violet and pink. . .

Since I have been here, the deserted garden, planted with large pines beneath which the grass grows tall and unkempt and mixed with various weeds, has sufficed for my work, and I have not yet gone outside. However, the country round Saint-Rémy is very beautiful and little by little I shall probably widen my field of endeavour.

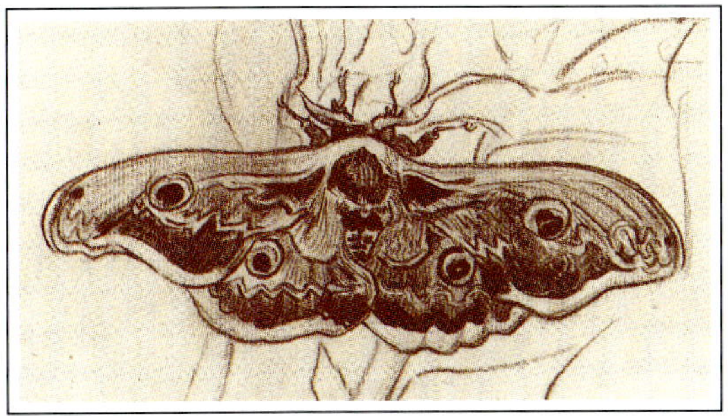

120 DEATH'S-HEAD MOTH
Vincent had to kill this moth in order to draw it. He marvelled at its beautiful colouring.

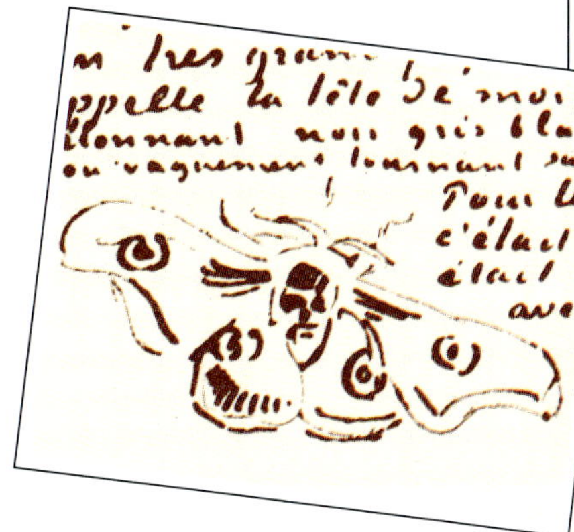

121 DEATH'S-HEAD MOTH
The markings on the moth's back suggest a human skull.

But if I stay here, the doctor will naturally be better able to see what is wrong, and will, I hope, be more reassured as to my being allowed to paint.

I *assure* you that I am quite all right here and that for the time being I see no reason at all for going to a boardinghouse in or near Paris. I have a little room with greenish-grey paper with two curtains of sea-green with a design of very pale roses, brightened by slight touches of blood-red.

These curtains, probably the relics of some rich and ruined deceased, are very pretty in design. A very worn armchair probably comes from the same source; it is upholstered with tapestry splashed over like a Diaz [nineteenth-century French painter] or a Monticelli, with brown, red, pink, white, cream, black, forget-me-not blue and bottle green. Through the iron-barred window I see a square field of wheat in an enclosure, a perspective like Van Goyen, above which I see the morning sun rising in all its glory. Besides this one—as there are more than thirty empty rooms—I have another one to work in.

The food is so-so. Naturally it tastes rather mouldy, like in a cockroach-infested restaurant in Paris or in a boardinghouse. As these poor souls do absolutely nothing (not a book, nothing to distract them but a game of bowls and a game of checkers) they have no other daily distraction than to stuff themselves with chick peas, beans, lentils, and other groceries and merchandise from the colonies in fixed quantities and at regular hours. . .

122 Fountain in the garden of the asylum
The fountain in front of the vestibule was to feature in many of Vincent's pictures of the peaceful walled garden.

123 Mountain landscape seen across the walls
Opposite: The view from Vincent's bedroom cell of the wheatfield and the Alpilles beyond. He painted this scene throughout the changing seasons.

The room where we stay on wet days is like a third-class waiting room in some stagnant village, the more so as there are some distinguished lunatics who always wear a hat, spectacles, and a cane, and travelling cloak, almost like at a watering place, and they represent the passengers.

Yesterday I drew a very big, rather rare night moth [120], called the death's head, its colouring of amazing distinction, black, grey, cloudy white tinged with carmine or vaguely shading off into olive-green; it is very big. I had to kill it to paint it, and it was a pity, the beastie was so beautiful. I will send you the drawing along with some other drawings of plants. . .

[592] Ever yours, Vincent

124 Brushes
Vincent was now far from any specialist shops and unable to buy his supplies. He wrote to Theo explaining the type of brushes he needed.

To Theo, c.2 June 1889

My dear Theo,

I must beg you again to send me some ordinary brushes, of about these sizes [124], as soon as possible. Half a dozen of each please . . .

When I have received the new canvas and the paints, I am going off to see a little of the country.

Since it is just the season when there are plenty of flowers and consequently colour effects, it would perhaps be wise to send me another five metres of canvas.

For the flowers are short-lived and will be replaced by the yellow wheatfields.

[593] Ever yours, Vincent

Vincent

125 OLIVE ORCHARD
Opposite: The first of Vincent's fifteen olive grove pictures done at Saint-Rémy.

To Theo, c.9 June 1889

MY DEAR THEO,

. . . What news can I tell you?—not much. I am working on two landscapes (size 30 canvases), views taken in the hills, one is the country that I see from the window of my bedroom [123]. In the foreground, a field of wheat ruined and hurled to the ground by a storm. A boundary wall and beyond the grey foliage of a few olive trees, some huts and the hills. Then at the top of the canvas a great white and grey cloud floating in the azure. It is a landscape of extreme simplicity in colouring too. . .

My health is all right, considering; I feel happier here with my work than I could be outside. By staying here a good long time, I shall have learned regular habits and in the long run the result will be more order in my life and less susceptibility. That will be so much to the good. Besides, I should not have the courage to begin again outside. I went once, still accompanied, to the village; the mere sight of people and things had such an effect on me that I thought I was going to faint and I felt very ill. . .

[594] Ever yours, Vincent

126 OLIVE TREES IN A MOUNTAIN LANDSCAPE
Vincent's drawing was made just outside the asylum walls, looking towards the Alpilles.

To Theo, 17 or 18 June 1889

MY DEAR THEO,

. . . I have a landscape with olive trees and also a new study of a starry sky [128].

[595] Ever yours, Vincent

127 CYPRESSES
A sketch of one of Vincent's paintings of cypresses.

128 THE STARRY NIGHT
Opposite: Vincent used the outline of the Alpilles from 'Mountain Landscape Seen across the Walls' [123] in his most intense painting from his year in Saint-Rémy.

To Theo, 25 June, 1889

MY DEAR THEO,

. . . The cypresses are always occupying my thoughts, I should like to make something of them like the canvases of the sunflowers, because it astonishes me that they have not yet been done as I see them.

It is as beautiful of line and proportion as an Egyptian obelisk.

And the green has a quality of such distinction.

It is a splash of *black* in a sunny landscape, but it is one of the most interesting black notes, and the most difficult to hit off exactly that I can imagine.

But then you must see them against the blue, *in* the blue rather. . .

I think that of the two canvases of cypresses, the one I am making this sketch of will be the best [127]. The trees in it are very big and massive. The foreground, very low with brambles and brushwood. Behind some violet hills, a green and pink sky with a crescent moon. The foreground especially is painted very thick, clumps of brambles with touches of yellow, violet and green. . .

[596] Ever yours, Vincent

To Theo, 2 July 1889

MY DEAR THEO,

. . . Thank you also very heartily for the Shakespeare. It will help me not to forget the little English I know, but above all is so fine. I have begun to read the series of which I knew least, which formerly, distracted by other things or not having the time, I could

129 Enclosed wheatfield with reaper
Opposite: The ripe wheat beneath his bedroom was ready for harvesting. For Vincent the reaper was also a symbol of death. He made two copies of the painting, this one for his mother.

not read; the series of the kings: I have already read *Richard II, Henry IV* and half of *Henry V*. I read without wondering if the ideas of the people of those times were different from our own, or what would become of them if you confronted them with republican and socialist beliefs and so on. But what touches me, as in some novelists of our day, is that the voices of these people, which in Shakespeare's case reach us from a distance of several centuries, do not seem unfamiliar to us. It is so much alive that you think you know them and see the thing. . .

The latest one [painting] I've started is the 'Wheatfield', in which there is a little reaper and a big sun [129]. It is all yellow except for the wall and the background of violet-tinted hills. The canvas which is almost the same in subject is different in colouring, being greyish-green with a white and blue sky. . .

[597] Ever yours, Vincent

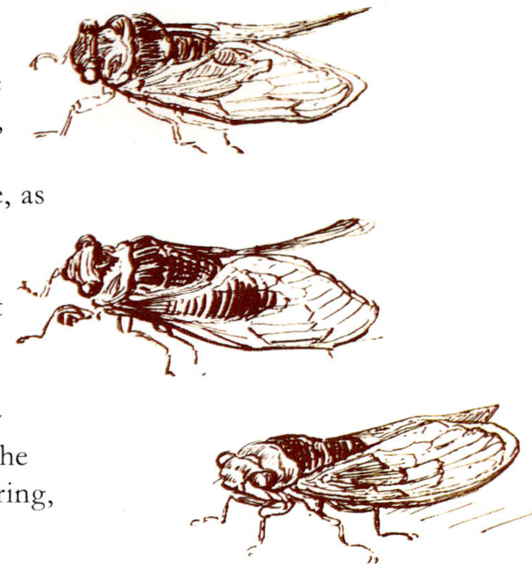

130 Cicadas
Vincent wrote of the grasshoppers, 'Their song in the great heat here has the same charm for me as the cricket on the hearth of the peasants at home.'

To Theo and Jo, 6 July 1889

My dear brother and sister,

Jo's letter told me a very great piece of news this morning, I congratulate you on it and I am very glad to hear it [Jo was pregnant]. . .

I am going to Arles tomorrow to get the canvases which are still there, and which I will send you soon. And I am going to send some of them as soon as possible to try to give you, even though you are in town, a peasant's thoughts.

This morning I talked a little with the doctor here—he told me exactly what I already thought—that I must wait a year before thinking myself cured, since the least little thing might bring on another attack. . .

[599] Ever yours, Vincent

Despair

Vincent suffered another relapse on 16 July 1889, two months after his arrival at Saint-Rémy. It was his longest breakdown, lasting five weeks. During this period he suffered agonizing hallucinations, he stopped painting and was unable to write. By September he had recovered enough to paint again. Painting comforted him, but he realized that there was unlikely to be a permanent cure.

The next breakdown came on Christmas Eve, exactly a year after he had mutilated his ear. Affected for a week, he tried to poison himself by eating his paints. Dr Peyron took them away, but a few days later they were returned and Vincent started a new series of pictures. His recovery was speedy and soon he was well enough to visit the ailing Madame Ginoux in Arles.

Two days after his return he suffered another short relapse. A month later Vincent returned again to Arles, but had a further breakdown and Dr Peyron had to send a carriage to Arles to bring him back. This was the worst relapse he had experienced and he did not recover until the end of April. But during this time he produced some of his saddest pictures: a series that he called 'memories of the North'. Vincent's suffering overshadowed the joy of Theo and Jo in Paris at the birth of their son, named Vincent Willem van Gogh, after his uncle.

By the beginning of May 1890 Vincent had recovered from his long breakdown and he was becoming increasingly restless. He talked of returning to the 'north', eventually deciding to move to the village of Auvers-sur-Oise, just outside Paris. During his last few weeks at the asylum he produced some of his best work and, in his final eighteen days, he finished eleven paintings.

131 OLD MAN WITH HIS HEAD ON HIS HANDS (AFTER THE LITHOGRAPH 'AT ETERNITY'S GATE')
Vincent made a painted copy of a print that he had done in The Hague more than six years earlier when he set out to become an artist. The original picture, captioned in English, shows a man patiently waiting for death.

To Theo, 22 August 1889

MY DEAR THEO,

. . .It would perhaps be a good thing if you wrote a few words to Dr. Peyron to tell him that working on my pictures is almost a necessity for my recovery, for these days without anything to do, and without being able to go to the room they had alloted me to do my painting in, are almost unbearable. . .

This new attack, my boy, came on me in the fields, on a windy day, when I was busy painting. I will send you the canvas. I finished it in spite of it.

And truly it was a more sober attempt, matt in colour without showing it, in broken greens, and reds and rusty yellow ochre, just as I told you that sometimes I felt a great desire to begin again with the same palette as in the North. . .

[601] Vincent

132 ENCLOSED FIELD WITH PLOUGHMAN
The sketch shows another of Vincent's paintings of the wheatfield outside his bedroom cell, this time being prepared for sowing.

To Theo, 3 or 4 September 1889

MY DEAR THEO,

. . .Yesterday I began to work a little again—on a thing that I see from my window—a field of yellow stubble that they are ploughing, the contrast of the violet-tinted ploughed earth with the strips of yellow stubble, background of hills [132].

Work distracts me infinitely better than anything else, and if I could once really throw myself into it with all my energy, possibly that would be the best remedy. . .

[602] Ever yours, Vincent

To Theo, 5 or 6 September 1889

MY DEAR THEO,

. . .I am working on two portraits of myself at this moment—for want of another model—because it is more than time I did a little figure work. One I began the day I got up; I was thin and pale as a ghost. It is dark violet-blue and the head whitish with yellow hair, so it has a colour effect.

But since then I have begun another one, three-quarter length on a light background [133]. . .

133 SELF-PORTRAIT
Vincent's most powerful self-portrait; the flaming background is evidence of the turmoil from which he had just emerged.

I am writing this letter little by little in the intervals when I am tired of painting. Work is going pretty well—I am struggling with a canvas begun some days before my indisposition, a 'Reaper'; the study is all yellow, terribly thickly painted, but the subject was fine and simple. For I see in this reaper—a vague figure fighting like a devil in the midst of the heat to get to the end of his task—I see in him the image of death, in the sense that humanity might be the wheat he is reaping. So it is—if you like—the opposite of that 'Sower' I tried to do before. But there's nothing sad in this death, it goes its way in broad daylight with a sun flooding everything with a light of pure gold [129]. . .

Yesterday I began the portrait of the head attendant, and perhaps I shall do his wife too, for he is married and lives in a little house a few steps away from the establishment. . . A very interesting face. . . altogether he is a man who has seen an enormous amount of suffering and death, and there is a sort of contemplative calm in his face [134]. . .

[604] Ever yours, Vincent

To Theo, 7 or 8 September 1889

MY DEAR THEO,

. . . During the attacks I feel a coward before the pain and suffering—more of a coward than I ought to be, and it is perhaps this very moral cowardice which, whereas I had no desire to get better before, makes me eat like two now, work hard, limit my relations with the other patients for fear of a relapse—altogether I am now trying to recover like a man who meant to commit suicide and, finding the water too cold, tries to regain the bank.

My dear brother, you know that I came to the South and threw myself into my work for a thousand reasons. Wishing to see a different light, thinking that looking at nature under a bright sky might give us a better idea of the Japanese way of feeling and drawing. Wishing also to see this stronger sun, because one feels that one could not understand Delacroix's pictures from the point of view of execution and technique without knowing it. . .

Sometimes religious thoughts bring me great consolation. So this last time during my illness an unfortunate accident happened to me—that lithograph of Delacroix's 'Pietà', along with some other sheets, fell into some oil and paint and was ruined.

I was very distressed—then in the meantime I have been busy painting it, and you will see it someday [135]. . .

[605] Ever yours, Vincent

134 PORTRAIT OF THE CHIEF ORDERLY (TRABUC).
Vincent made a copy of his painting of the 59-year-old Charles Trabuc for Theo.

To Wil, 19 September 1889

MY DEAR SISTER,

. . . It is splendid weather outside—but for a long time—two months to be exact—I have not left my room; I don't know why.

What I need is courage, and this often fails me. And it is also a fact that since my disease, when I am in the fields I am overwhelmed by a feeling of loneliness to such a horrible extent that I shy away from going out. But this will change all the same as time goes on. Only when I stand a painting before my easel do I feel somewhat alive. Never mind, this is going to change too, for now my health is so good that I suppose the physical part of me will gain the victory.

I embrace you in thought, and 'see you soon!'

[W14] Yours, Vincent

135 PIETÀ (AFTER DELACROIX)
This was the first of Vincent's series of copies of works by his favourite artists, in which he translated their prints into his own painted versions.

To Theo, c.8 October 1889

MY DEAR THEO,

. . . I am feeling well just now. I think M. Peyron is right when he says that I am not strictly speaking mad, for my mind is absolutely normal in the intervals, and even more so than before. But during the attacks it is terrible—and then I lose consciousness of everything. But that spurs me on to work and to seriousness, like a miner who is always in danger makes haste in what he does. . .

[610] Ever yours, Vincent

To Anna, 20–22 October 1889

MY DEAR MOTHER,

. . . Though I saw Paris and other big cities for many years, I keep looking more or less like a peasant of Zundert [Vincent's birthplace]. . . and sometimes I imagine I also feel and think like

them, only the peasants are of more use in the world. Only when they have all the other things, they get a feeling, a desire for pictures, books, etc. In my estimation I consider myself certainly below the peasants.

Well, I am ploughing on my canvases as they do on their fields.

It goes badly enough in our profession—in fact that has always been so, but at the moment it is very bad.

And yet never have such high prices been paid for pictures as these days.

What makes us work on is friendship for each other, and love of nature, and finally, if one has taken all the pains to master the brush, *one cannot leave painting alone*. Compared with others, I still belong to the lucky ones, but think what it must be if one has entered the profession and has to leave it before one has done anything, and there are many like that. Given ten years as necessary to learn the profession and somebody who has struggled through six years and paid for them and then has to stop, just think how miserable that is, and how many there are like that!

And those high prices one hears about, paid for work of painters who are dead and who were never paid so much while they were alive, it is a kind of tulip trade, under which the living painters suffer. . . And it will also disappear like the tulip trade.

But one may reason that, though the tulip trade has long been gone and is forgotten, the flower growers have remained and will remain. . .

[612] Your loving Vincent

To Wil, c.20–22 October 1889

MY DEAR SISTER,

. . . You will probably think the interior of the empty bedroom with a wooden bedstead and two chairs the most unbeautiful thing

of all—and notwithstanding this I have painted it twice, on a large scale [71].

I wanted to achieve an effect of simplicity of the sort one finds described in *Felix Holt* [George Eliot's novel]. After being told this you may quickly understand this picture, but it will probably remain ridiculous in the eyes of others who have not been warned. Doing a simple thing with bright colours is not at all easy. . .

[W15] Yours, Vincent

To Bernard, c.20 November 1889

MY DEAR FRIEND BERNARD,

. . . Last year you did a picture—according to what Gauguin told me—which I think was something like this: on a grassy foreground a figure of a young girl in a blue or whitish dress, lying stretched out full length; on the second plane the edge of a beech wood, the ground covered with fallen red leaves, the verdigris-coloured tree trunks forming a vertical barrier.

I suppose the hair is an accent of a colour tone which is necessary as a colour complementary to the pale dress, black if the dress is white, orange if it is blue. But what I said to myself was, what a simple subject, and how well he knows how to create elegance with nothing.

Gauguin told me about another subject, nothing but three trees, an effect of orange foliage against a blue sky; but then very clearly designed, and very categorically divided into planes of contrasting and candid colours—bravo!. . .

If I have not written you for a long while, it is because. . . I had to struggle against my illness. . .

Here is the description of a canvas which is in front of me at the moment [136]. A view of the park of the asylum where I am staying; on the right a grey terrace and a side wall of the house.

Some deflowered rose bushes, on the left a stretch of the park—red-ochre—the soil scorched by the sun, covered with fallen pine needles. This edge of the park is planted with large pine trees, whose trunks and branches are red-ochre, the foliage green gloomed over by an admixture of black. These high trees stand out against an evening sky with violet stripes on a yellow ground, which higher up turns into pink, into green. A wall—also red-ochre—shuts off the view, and is topped only by a violet and yellow-ochre hill. Now the nearest tree is an enormous trunk, struck by lightning and sawed off. But one side branch shoots up very high and lets fall an avalanche of dark green pine needles. This sombre giant—like a defeated proud man—contrasts, when considered in the nature of a living creature, with the pale smile of a last rose on the fading bush in front of him. Underneath the trees, empty stone benches, sullen box trees; the sky is mirrored—yellow—in a puddle left by the rain. A sunbeam, the last ray of daylight, raises the sombre ochre almost to orange. Here and there small black figures wander around among the tree trunks. . .

136 A CORNER OF THE ASYLUM AND THE GARDEN WITH A HEAVY, SAWED-OFF TREE
Vincent looked out at this tree from his studio window.

[B21] Sincerely yours, Vincent

To Theo, c.21 November 1889

MY DEAR THEO,

I have to thank you very much for a package of paints, which was accompanied by an excellent woolen waistcoat.

How kind you are to me, and how I wish I could do something good, so as to prove to you that I would like to be less ungrateful. The paints reached me at the right moment, because what I had brought back from Arles was almost exhausted. The thing is that this month I have been working in the olive groves. . .

The olive is as variable as our willow or pollard willow in the North, you know the willows are very striking, in spite of their seeming monotonous, they are the trees characteristic of the country. Now the olive and the cypress have exactly the significance here as the willow has at home. . .

[615] Ever yours, Vincent

To Theo, 7 December 1889

MY DEAR THEO,

. . .I have gone on working outside till now in spite of the cold, and I think it is doing me good, and the work too.

The last study I did is a view of the village, where they were at work—under some enormous plane trees—repairing the pavements [111]. So there are heaps of sand, stones and the gigantic trunks—the leaves yellowing and here and there you get a glimpse of a house front and small figures.

[618] Ever yours, Vincent

To Anna, c.20 December 1889

MY DEAR MOTHER,

Toward the end of the year I come once more to say good day to you—you will say that I have forgotten that several times. It is a year since I fell ill, and it is difficult for me to say how far I have

or have not recovered. I often feel much self-reproach about things in the past, my illness being more or less my own fault, in any case I doubt if I can make up for faults in any way.

But reasoning and thinking about these things is sometimes so difficult, and sometimes my feelings overwhelm me more than before. . .

And now I wish you a happy Christmas and a good Old and New Year's Eve.

An embrace in thought from,

[619] Your loving Vincent

To Joseph-Michel and Marie Ginoux, 30 or 31 December 1889

MY DEAR FRIENDS, MONSIEUR AND MADAME GINOUX,

I do not know whether you remember—I think it rather strange that it is nearly a year since Madame Ginoux was taken ill at the same time as myself. . . So, my dear friends, as now and then we suffer together, this makes me think of what Madame Ginoux said—'When you are friends, you are friends for a long time. . .' Personally I believe that the adversities one meets with in the ordinary course of life do us as much good as harm. The very complaint that makes one ill today, overwhelming one with discouragement, that same thing—once the disease has passed off—gives us the energy to get up and to want to be completely recovered tomorrow.

I assure you that last year I almost hated the idea of regaining my health—of only feeling somewhat better for a shorter or longer time—always living in fear of relapses—I almost hated the idea, I tell you—so little did I feel inclined to begin again. Often I said to myself that I preferred that there be nothing further, that this be the end. Ah, well—it would seem that we are not the masters of this—of our existence—it seems that what matters is

that one should learn to want to go on living, even when suffering. Oh, I feel so cowardly in this respect; even when my health has returned, I am still afraid. So who am I to encourage others, you will say, for actually this is hardly my style. Well, it is only to tell you, my dear friends, that I hope so ardently, and even dare believe, that Madame Ginoux's illness will be of very short duration, and that she will rise from her sickbed a much stronger fellow, but she knows only too well how fond we all are of her. . . In my case my disease has done me good—it would be ungrateful not to acknowledge it. It has made me easier in my mind. . .

[622a] Ever yours, Vincent

To Theo, 1 or 2 January 1890

MY DEAR BROTHER,

. . .First of all I wish you and Jo a happy New Year and regret that I have perhaps, though quite unwillingly, caused you worry, because M. Peyron must have informed you that my mind has once more been deranged. . .

Odd that I had been working perfectly calmly on some canvases that you will soon see, and that suddenly, without any reason, the aberration seized me again.

I do not know what M. Peyron is going to advise, but while taking what he tells me into account, I think that he will dare less than ever to commit himself as to the possibility of my living as I used to. It is to be feared that the attacks will return. But that is no reason at all for not trying to distract oneself a little.

For cooping up all these lunatics in this old cloister becomes, I think, a dangerous thing, in which you risk losing the little good sense that you may still have kept. . .

[620] Ever yours, Vincent

To Jo, 31 January 1890

MY DEAR JO,

It moves me so much that you write to me and are so calm and master of yourself on one of your difficult nights [awaiting the birth of her baby]. How I am longing to get the news that you have come safely through, and that your child is living. How happy Theo will be, and a new sun will rise inside him when he sees you recovering. . .

[624] Your brother, Vincent

137 PRISONERS' ROUND (AFTER GUSTAVE DORÉ) *Doré's print of 'Newgate: the Exercise Yard' must have reminded Vincent of life at the asylum. The man in the centre, with the red hair, may be a self-portrait.*

To Theo, 2 February 1890

MY DEAR THEO,

Today I received your good news that you are at last a father, that the most critical time is over for Jo, and finally that the little boy is well. That has done me more good and given me more pleasure than I can put into words. Bravo—and how pleased Mother is going to be. The day before yesterday I received a fairly long and very contented letter from her too. Anyhow, here it is, the thing I have so much desired for such a long time. No need to tell you that I have often thought of you these days, and it touched me very much that Jo had the kindness to write to me the very night before. She was so brave and calm in her danger, it moved me deeply. Well, it contributes a great deal to helping me forget the last days when I was ill. . .

[625] Ever yours, Vincent

To Anna, c.20 February 1890

MY DEAR MOTHER,

. . .I imagine that, like me, your thoughts are much with Jo and Theo: how glad I was when the news came that it had ended well: it was a good thing that Wil stayed on. I should have greatly preferred him to call the boy after Father, of whom I have been thinking so much these days, instead of after me; but seeing it has now been done, I started right away to make a picture for him, to hang in their bedroom, big branches of white almond blossom against a blue sky [138]. . .

[627] Your loving Vincent

138 BRANCHES OF AN ALMOND TREE IN BLOSSOM
Vincent painted this symbol of new life to celebrate the birth of his nephew. The day after he finished the picture he suffered a further breakdown.

To Theo, 24 April 1890

MY DEAR THEO,

Today I wanted to read the letters which had come for me, but I was not clear-headed enough yet to be able to understand them.

However, I am trying to answer you at once, and I hope that this will clear away in a few days. Above all I hope that you are well, and your wife and child too. Don't worry about me, even if this should last a bit longer. . .

Remember me to Gauguin, who wrote me a letter for which I thank him very, very much; I am terribly dazed in the head, but must try to be patient. . .

Ever yours, Vincent

I take up this letter again to try to write, it will come little by little, the thing is that my head is so bad, without pain it is true, but altogether stupefied. . .

My work was going well, the last canvas of branches in blossom —you will see that it was perhaps the best, the most patiently worked thing I had done, painted with calm and with a greater firmness of touch [138]. And the next day, down like a brute. . .

[628]

To Theo, 29 or 30 April 1890

My dear Theo,

Until now I have not been able to write you, but being a bit better just now, I did not wish to delay wishing you a happy year, since it's your birthday [Theo would be 33 on 1 May]. . .

What am I to say about these last two months? Things didn't go well at all. I am sadder and more wretched than I can say, and I do not know at all where I have got to.

The order for paints is rather big [139], so let me wait for half of it if it is more convenient to you.

While I was ill I nevertheless did some little canvases from memory which you will see later, memories of the North. . .

I felt ill at the time I was doing the almond blossoms [138]. If I had been able to go on working, you can judge from it that I would have done others of trees in blossom. Now the trees in blossom are almost over, really I have no luck. Yes, I must try to get out of here, but where to go?. . .

[629] Ever yours, Vincent

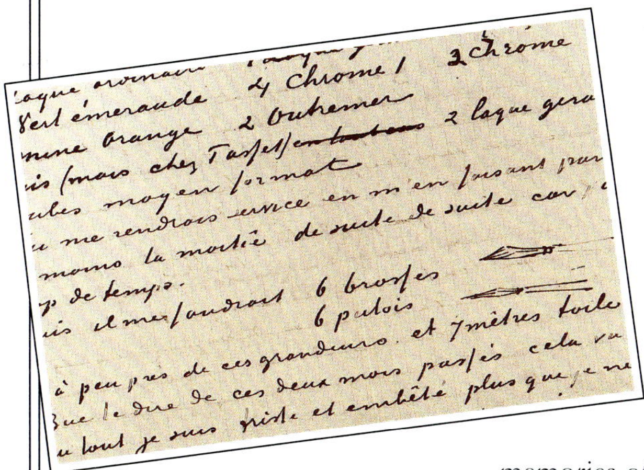
laque ordinaire 2 Chrôme
Vert émeraude 4 Chrome 1
mine orange 2 Outremer
is (mais chez Tasset/~~en tubes~~ 2 laque gera
ules moyen format
u me rendrois service en m'en faisant par
moins la moitié de suite de suite car
p de temps.
is il me faudrait 6 brosses
6 putois
à peu près de ces grandeurs. et 7 mètres toile
que le dire de ces deux mois passés cela va
u tout je suis triste et embêté plus que je ne

139 Letter to Theo
29 or 30 April 1890. Vincent described the brushes that he wanted his brother to send.

140 THE RAISING OF LAZARUS (AFTER A DETAIL FROM AN ENGRAVING BY REMBRANDT)
Vincent, in making a free interpretation of a detail of the print, added the sun in both the painting and the sketch [141].

To Theo, 3 May 1890

MY DEAR THEO,

I write once more to tell you that I continue to be in good health, however, I feel rather exhausted by this long attack. . .

The etchings which you sent me are very fine! On the back of this page I have scribbled a sketch after a painting I have done of three figures which are in the background of the etching of 'Lazarus' [by Rembrandt]: the dead man and his two sisters [140]. The cave and the corpse are white-yellow-violet. The woman who takes the handkerchief away from the face of the resurrected man has a green dress and orange hair, the other has black hair and a gown of striped green and pink. . .

[632] Ever yours, Vincent

142 FIELD OF GRASS WITH DANDELIONS AND TREE TRUNKS
A sketch of the first painting Vincent did after his longest breakdown, a scene from the asylum garden.

To Theo, 4 May 1890

MY DEAR THEO,

. . .I warned you nearly six months ago that if I had another attack of the same nature, I should wish to change my asylum. . .

My surroundings here begin to weigh on me more than I can say—my word, I have been patient for more than a year—I need air, I feel overwhelmed with boredom and grief. . .

I can't go on, I am at the end of my patience, my dear brother, I can't stand any more—I must make a change, even a desperate one.

However, there really is a chance that the change will do me good—my work is going well, I have done two canvases of the fresh grass in the park, one of which is extremely simple, here is a hasty sketch of it [142]. . .

Ever yours, Vincent

[631]

To Theo, 11 or 12 May 1890

MY DEAR BROTHER,

. . .I am working to give a last stroke of the brush here with a calm and steady enthusiasm. I am doing a canvas of roses with a light green background and two canvases representing big bunches of violet irises, one lot against a pink background in which the effect is soft and harmonious because of the combination of greens, pinks, violets [143]. On the other hand, the other violet bunch (ranging from carmine to pure Prussian blue) stands out against a startling citron background, with other yellow tones in the vase and the stand on which it rests, so it is an effect of tremendously

143 Vase with violet irises against a pink background
Vincent painted the irises in a vase almost a year after he had depicted them growing in the asylum garden.

disparate complementaries, which strengthen each other by their juxtaposition. . .

The day of my departure depends on when I'm packed and have finished my canvases; I am working on the latter with such enthusiasm that packing seems to me more difficult than painting. Anyway, it won't be long. . .

[633] Ever yours, Vincent

To Joseph-Michel Ginoux, 11 or 12 May 1890

My dear Monsieur Ginoux,

. . .I greatly regret I fell ill on the day I came to Arles to say good-bye to you all—after that I was ill for two months without being

able to work. However, at present I am quite well again.
But I am going to return to the North, and so, my dear friends, I vigorously shake your hands in thought, as well as the hands of the neighbours, and believe me when I say that over there I shall often think of you all, for what Madame Ginoux said is true—if you are friends, you are friends for a long time. If you should happen to see the Roulins, you will surely not forget to remember me to them.

So I stop for now, hoping that Madame Ginoux has quite recovered from her indisposition, and with another handshake,

I am

[634a] Sincerely yours, Vincent

144 *Sketch of* Road with Men Walking, Carriage, Cypress, Star and Crescent Moon
Vincent sketched his final Saint-Rémy painting in a letter to Gauguin.

To Theo, 13 May 1890

My dear brother,

After a last discussion with Monsieur Peyron, I have permission to pack, and have sent my luggage by goods train. The 30 kilos of luggage which one may carry will be enough for me to bring some frames, the easel and stretchers, etc., with me. I shall leave as soon as you write to Monsieur Peyron. I feel quite calm and I do not think that in my present condition I shall be easily upset.

In any case I hope to be in Paris before Sunday. . .

I feel my head is absolutely calm for my work, and the brush strokes come to me and follow each other logically. Anyway, till Sunday at the latest, I shake your hand. . . kindest regards to Jo.

[634] Ever yours, Vincent

145 ROAD WITH MEN WALKING, CARRIAGE, CYPRESS, STAR, AND CRESCENT MOON
A strongly expressionist picture from Vincent's imagination; it was the last painting that he did at Saint-Rémy.

· POSTSCRIPT : AUVERS ·

Vincent left Provence, after a year at Saint-Rémy, to go to Auvers-sur-Oise, a village near Paris where he could be closer to Theo. It was here that he ended his life, shooting himself in the wheatfields.

146 COTTAGES WITH THATCHED ROOFS AND FIGURES
Opposite: A row of houses in the rue du Gré, in the hamlet of Chaponval near Auvers.

147 *SKETCH OF* COTTAGES WITH THATCHED ROOFS AND FIGURES
This sketch was contained in Vincent's last letter to Theo.

Vincent arrived in Paris on 17 May 1890 to be greeted at the station by his brother. Theo took him to their new flat at 8 Cité Pigalle, where Vincent met Jo and their four-month-old son. After the tranquility of the asylum, the bustle of the outside world made Vincent uneasy and four days later he set off for the village of Auvers-sur-Oise.

Auvers, an attractive village twenty miles north of Paris, had been suggested by the painter Camille Pissarro, who had explained that his friend the physician Dr Paul Gachet could keep an eye on Vincent. When he heard of the idea Vincent was enthusiastic, particularly because Auvers had been the home of the painter Charles-François Daubigny and both Pissarro and Cézanne had worked there.

Auvers was a straggling village situated in the narrow valley of the River Oise, overlooked by wheatfields on the plateau above. It was still a rural community of farmers, but the railway had recently opened up the area making it easily accessible to visitors from Paris. For Vincent, it seemed an ideal location, close enough to his brother, yet removed from the distractions of Paris and, most important, it provided plenty of subjects to paint. With the arrival of spring, Vincent's hopes were high.

Vincent's first two months in Auvers went well. He worked with great intensity, completing on average a painting each day. He left Auvers for the first time on 6 July, when he went by train to visit Theo and Jo in Paris. Sadly, it was a day full of tensions: baby Vincent was ill and Theo was so frustrated with his work at the Boussod & Valadon Gallery that his thoughts were full of leaving to set up his own business. On Vincent's return to Auvers, his letters become increasingly tense. Vincent's mind was now in turmoil. On 27 July 1890 he climbed up to the wheatfields above Auvers that he had painted so often and shot himself in the stomach, wounding himself badly. He trudged back to the Café Ravoux and climbed up the stairs to his room in the attic. Two days later the artist was dead.

148 LANDSCAPE IN THE RAIN
The village of Auvers, with the wheatfields above.

To Theo and Jo, 20 May 1890

My dear Theo and dear Jo,

. . . Auvers is very beautiful, among other things a lot of old thatched roofs, which are getting rare. So I should hope that by settling down to do some canvases of this there would be a chance of recovering the expenses of my stay—for really it is profoundly beautiful, it is the real country, characteristic and picturesque.

I have seen Dr Gachet, who gives me the impression of being rather eccentric, but his experience as a doctor must keep him balanced enough to combat the nervous trouble from which he certainly seems to me to be suffering at least as seriously as I.

He piloted me to an inn where they ask 6 francs a day. All by myself I found one where I shall pay 3.50 francs a day.

And I think I ought to stay there until a new arrangement is made. When I have done some studies, I shall see if it would be better to move, but it seems unfair to me, when you are willing and able to pay and work like any other labourer, to have to pay almost double because you work at painting. Anyway, I am going to the inn at 3.50 first. . .

In Paris I felt very strongly that all the noise there was not for me.

I am so glad to have seen Jo and the little one and your apartment, which is certainly better than the other one.

Wishing you good luck and good health and hoping to see you again soon, a good handshake,

Vincent

[635]

149 Portrait of Dr Gachet
Vincent's friend Dr Gachet practised homeopathic medicine and used foxglove for treating heart diseases. This version was painted for him at his request.

To Theo, 3 June 1890

MY DEAR THEO,

. . . Gachet [and I]. . . are great friends already. . .

I am working at his portrait, the head with a white cap, very fair, very light, the hands also a light flesh tint, a blue frock coat and a cobalt blue background, leaning on a red table, on which are a yellow book and a foxglove plant with purple flowers [150].

Monsieur Gachet is absolutely *fanatical* about this portrait, and wants me to do one for him, if I can, exactly like it [149]. I should like to myself. . . He always comes back to these two portraits when he comes to see the studies, and he understands them exactly. . .

I hope to send you a portrait of him soon. Then I have painted two studies at his house. . . an aloe with marigolds and cypresses, then last Sunday some white roses, vines and a white figure in it.

I shall most probably also do the portrait of his daughter, who is nineteen years old, and with whom I imagine Jo would soon be friends [153].

Then I am looking forward to doing the portraits of all of you in the open air; yours, Jo's and the little one's. . .

[638] From Vincent

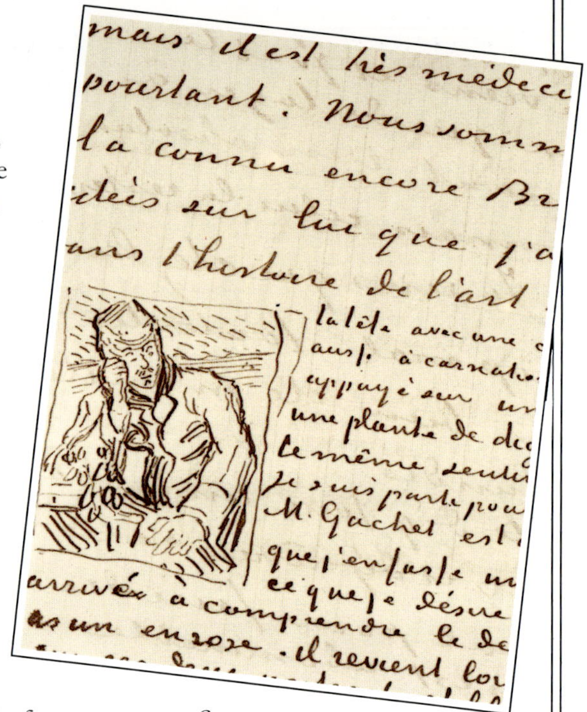
mais il est très médec
pourtant. Nous somm
l'a connu encore Br
idées sur lui que j'a
ans l'histoire de l'art
la tête avec une
aussi à carnation
appuyé sur un
une plante de dig
le même senti
je suis parti pour
M. Gachet est
que j'en fasse un
ce que je désire
arrivé à comprendre le de
as un encore. il revient tou

150 SKETCH OF DOCTOR GACHET SITTING AT A TABLE WITH BOOKS AND A GLASS WITH SPRIGS OF FOXGLOVE
Vincent sent Theo a little sketch of his portrait of Dr Gachet.

To Anna, 4 June 1890

MY DEAR MOTHER,

. . . Time passes quickly, though some days last long. In fact, I did not intend to return to Paris so soon; I should have stayed in

151 THE CHURCH IN AUVERS
Seven weeks after Vincent painted this picture, the church refused to hold his funeral service there because he had taken his own life.

Saint-Rémy another year if I had not attributed my last attack partly to the influence which the illness of others had on me, for which reason I decided it was time to change my surroundings if I wanted to keep my energy . . .

[639] Your loving Vincent

To Wil, c.5 June 1890

MY DEAR SISTER,

I ought long ago to have replied to the two letters I received when I was still at Saint-Rémy, but the journey, the work and a lot of new emotions caused me to postpone from day to day until this moment writing you a letter. . .

I have found a true friend in Dr Gachet, something like another brother, so much do we resemble each other physically and also mentally. He is a very nervous man himself and very queer in his behaviour; he has extended much friendliness to the artists of the new school, and he has helped them as much as was in his power. I painted his portrait the other day, and I am also going to paint a portrait of his daughter, who is nineteen years old [153]. He lost his wife some years ago, which greatly contributed to his becoming a broken man. I believe I may say we have been friends from the very first, and every week I shall go stay at his house one

or two days in order to work in his garden, where I have already painted two studies, one with southern plants, aloes, cypresses, marigolds; the other with white roses, some vines and a figure, and a cluster of ranunculuses besides. Apart from these I have a larger picture of the village church—an effect in which the building appears to be violet-hued against a sky of a simple deep blue colour, pure cobalt; the stained-glass windows appear as ultramarine blotches, the roof is violet and partly orange [151]. In the foreground some green plants in bloom, and sand with the pink glow of sunshine on it. . .

[W22] Yours, Vincent

To Joseph-Michel and Marie Ginoux, c.*12 June 1890*

My dear friends Ginoux,

Yes, I too was very sorry that I could not return to Arles to say good-bye to you all, for you know well that I had become attached to the people and things of your town with a sincere friendship. But lately I had contracted the other patients' disease to such an extent that I could not be cured of mine. The other patients' society had a bad influence on me, and in the end I was absolutely unable to understand it. Then I felt I had better try a change, and for that matter, the pleasure of seeing my brother, his family and my painter friends again has done me a lot of good, and I am feeling completely calm and normal. The doctor here says that I ought to throw myself into my work. . . and so distract my mind. . .

But still I often think of you all, one cannot do what one wants in life. The more you feel attached to a spot, the more ruthlessly you are compelled to leave it, but the memories remain, and one remembers—as in a looking glass, darkly—one's absent friends. . .

[640a] Cordially yours, Vincent van Gogh

To Gauguin, 17 June 1890

My dear friend Gauguin,

Thank you for having written to me again, old fellow, and rest assured that since my return I have thought of you every day. I stayed in Paris only three days, and the noise, etc., of Paris had such a bad effect on me that I thought it wise for my head's sake to fly to the country; but for that, I should soon have dropped in on you.

And it gives me enormous pleasure when you say the Arlésienne's portrait, which was based strictly on your drawing, is to your liking [91]. I tried to be religiously faithful to your drawing [14], while nevertheless taking the liberty of interpreting through the medium of colour the sober character and the style of the drawing in question. It is a synthesis of the Arlésiennes, if you like; as syntheses of the Arlésiennes are rare, take this as a work belonging to you and me as a summary of our months of work together. For my part I paid for doing it with another month of illness, but I also know that it is a canvas which will be understood by you, and by a very few others, as we would wish it to be understood. My friend Dr Gachet has taken to it altogether after two or three hesitations and says, 'How difficult it is to be simple.'

I still have a cypress with a star from down there, a last attempt—a night sky with a moon without radiance, the slender crescent barely emerging from the opaque shadow cast by the earth—one star with an exaggerated brilliance, if you like, a soft brilliance of pink and green in the ultramarine sky, across which some clouds are hurrying. Below, a road bordered with tall yellow canes, behind these the blue *Basses Alpes*, an old inn with yellow lighted windows, and a very tall cypress, very straight, very sombre. . .

152 Ears of wheat
Vincent's sketch shows the swirling pattern of ripening wheat.

Look, here's an idea which may suit you, I am trying to do some studies of wheat like this, but I cannot draw it—nothing but ears of wheat with green-blue stalks, long leaves like ribbons of green shot with pink, ears that are just turning yellow, edged with the pale pink of the dusty bloom—a pink bindweed at the bottom twisted round a stem [152]. . .

[643]

[This unfinished letter was found with Vincent's papers after his death.]

153 Marguerite Gachet at the Piano
Marguerite was the daughter of Dr Gachet.

To Theo, 28 June 1890

My dear Theo,

You should send the enclosed order for paints at the beginning of the month, anyway at the most convenient time, there is no hurry, a few days sooner or later don't matter.

Yesterday and the day before I painted Mlle Gachet's portrait, which I hope you will see soon; the dress is red, the wall in the background green with orange spots, the carpet red with green spots, the piano dark violet; it is 40 inches high by 20 inches wide.

It is a figure that I enjoyed painting—but it is difficult. He has promised to make her pose for me another time at the small organ. I will do one for you—I have noticed that this canvas goes very well with another horizontal one of wheat, as one canvas is vertical and in pink tones, the other pale green and greenish-yellow, the complementary of pink; but we are still far from the time when people will understand the curious relation between one fragment of nature and another, which all the same explain each other and enhance each other. But some certainly feel it, and that's something. . .

[645] Ever yours, Vincent

154 Drawing of Marguerite Gachet at the Piano
A chalk drawing of Dr Gachet's daughter, which was probably a preliminary study for the painting.

155 Couple walking between rows of trees
The two lovers are probably strolling through the grounds of the château of Auvers.

To Theo and Jo, c.7 July 1890

MY DEAR BROTHER AND SISTER,

My impression is that since we are all rather distressed and a little overwrought besides, it matters comparatively little to insist on having any very clear definition of the position in which we are. You rather surprise me by seeming to wish to force the situation. Can I do anything about it, at least can I do anything that you would like me to do?

However that may be, once again, a good handshake in thought, and in spite of everything, it gave me great pleasure to see you all again.

Be very sure of that.

[647] Ever yours, Vincent

[This letter was not sent. It was folded and must have been carried in Vincent's pocket.]

156 *SKETCH OF* COUPLE WALKING BETWEEN ROWS OF TREES
This sketch of a painting of two lovers was sent to Theo and his new wife Jo.

To Theo and Jo, c.10 July 1890

MY DEAR BROTHER AND SISTER,

. . . Back here, I still felt very sad and continued to feel the storm which threatens you weighing on me too. What was to be done you see, I generally try to be fairly cheerful, but my life is also threatened at the very root, and my steps are also wavering.

I feared—not altogether but yet a little—that being a burden to you, you felt me to be rather a thing to be dreaded, but Jo's letter proves to me clearly that you understand that for my part I am as much in toil and trouble as you are.

There—once back here I set to work again—though the brush almost slipped from my fingers, but knowing exactly what I wanted, I have painted three more big canvases since.

They are vast fields of wheat under troubled skies, and I did not need to go out of my way to try to express sadness and extreme loneliness [157, 158]. I hope you will see them soon—for I hope to bring them to you in Paris as soon as possible, since I almost think that these canvases will tell you what I cannot say in words, the health and restorative forces that I see in the country . . .

I hope with all my heart that the intended journey will give you a little distraction.

I often think of the little one. I think it is certainly better to bring up children than to give all your nervous energy to making pictures, but what then, I am—at least I feel—too old to retrace my steps or to desire anything different. That desire has left me, though the mental suffering of it remains.

157 Wheatfields
Vincent's favourite view across the plains of Auvers. It was close to here that he took his life.

[649] Ever yours, Vincent

To Theo, 24 July 1890

My dear brother,

Thanks for your letter of today and the 50-fr. note it contained.

Perhaps I'd rather write you about a lot of things, but to begin with, the desire to do so has completely left me, and then I feel it is useless.

I hope that you will have found those worthy gentlemen well disposed towards you.

As far as I'm concerned, I apply myself to my canvases with all my mind, I am trying to do as well as certain painters whom I have greatly loved and admired.

Now I'm back, what I think is that the painters themselves are fighting more and more with their backs to the wall. Very well. . . but isn't the moment for trying to make them understand the usefulness of a union already gone? On the other hand a union, if it should take shape, would founder if the rest should have to founder. Then perhaps you would say that some dealers might combine on behalf of the Impressionists, but that would be very short-lived. Altogether I think that personal initiative remains powerless, and having had experience of it, should we start again?

158 *SKETCH OF* WHEATFIELDS
Vincent sketched the painting he had made of the view above Auvers. The sketch, which depicted the fields where he was to take his life, was included in his last letter to Theo.

I noticed with pleasure that the Gauguin from Brittany which I saw was very beautiful, and I think that the others he has done there must be so too.

Perhaps you will look at this sketch of Daubigny's garden. It is one of my most purposeful canvases. I add a sketch of some old thatched roofs and the sketches of two size 30 canvases representing vast fields of wheat after the rain [157, 158]. . .

Good-bye now, and good luck in business, etc., remember me to Jo and handshakes in thought.

[651] Ever yours, Vincent

To Theo, 24 July 1890

MY DEAR BROTHER,

Thanks for your kind letter and for the 50-franc note it contained.

There are many things I should like to write you about, but I feel it is useless. I hope you have found those worthy gentlemen favourably disposed toward you.

Your reassuring me as to the peacefulness of your household was hardly worth the trouble, I think, having seen the weal and woe of it for myself. And I quite agree with you that rearing a boy on a fourth floor is a hell of a job for you as well as for Jo.

Since the thing that matters most is going well, why should I say more about things of less importance? My word, before we have a chance to talk business more collectedly, we shall probably have a long way to go.

The other painters, whatever they think, instinctively keep themselves at a distance from discussions about the actual trade.

Well, the truth is, we can only make our pictures speak. But yet, my dear brother, there is this that I have always told you, and I repeat it once more with all the earnestness that can be expressed by the effort of a mind diligently fixed on trying to do as well as possible—I tell you again that I shall always consider you to be something more than a simple dealer in Corots, that through my mediation you have your part in the actual production of some canvases, which will retain their calm even in the catastrophe.

For this is what we have got to, and this is all or at least the main thing that I can have to tell you at a moment of comparative crisis. At a moment when things are very strained between dealers in pictures of dead artists, and living artists.

Well, my own work, I am risking my life for it and my reason has half foundered because of it—that's all right—but you are not among the dealers in men as far as I know, and you can still choose your side, I think, acting with humanity, but what do you want?

[652]

[This unfinished letter was never sent, and was found on Vincent's body after he shot himself. It must have been a draft for the previous letter.]

159 Wheatfield under threatening skies with crows
With all three paths ending abruptly, there is a brooding sense of menace in this picture.

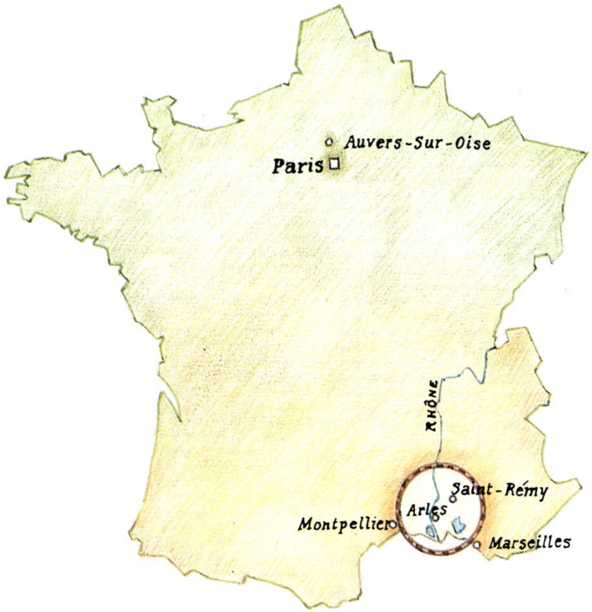

VINCENT VAN GOGH'S

PROVENCE

In the Footsteps of Vincent van Gogh: A Travel Guide

ARLES

Arles is an attractive Roman town, and the centre has changed relatively little since Vincent's day. The place du Forum, on the site of the Roman forum, is where Vincent painted his 'Café Terrace at Night', in which the brightly-lit terrace is set against a deep blue starry sky. The small square is still edged by cafés, although the one immortalized by Vincent has become a furniture shop (above it is an excellent restaurant, Le Vaccarès).

Close to the forum is the Roman arena, the largest surviving amphitheatre in Gaul, from the top of which there is an excellent view of the town. Vincent often went to the Sunday bullfights, which continue to be held during the summer. He once painted the scene, concentrating on the spectators rather than the dramatic Roman architecture. He also painted the Alyscamps, the avenue of ancient tombs just beyond the ramparts to the southeast. It remains a charming place to stroll, seemingly untouched by the modern world.

Vincent was never a 'tourist'. Only once in his letters does he mention the medieval church of Saint-Trophîme (place de la République), describing the sculpted figures on the Romanesque portal as 'so cruel, like a Chinese nightmare'. He dismissed the town's art museum (rue du Grand Prieuré), devoted to the local artist Jacques Réattu, as 'a horror and a humbug'. The most interesting museum in Arles was not established until 1896, a few years after Vincent's stay, by the Provençal poet Frédéric Mistral (rue de la République). Crowded with treasures and with junk, the Arlaten Museum gives a vivid impression of Arles in the late nineteenth century.

The Hôtel Carrel (30 rue Cavalerie), where Vincent stayed for his first two months in Arles, was destroyed during the Second World War. His next lodging, the Café de la Gare (30 place Lamartine), was also bombed as was his studio at the Yellow House (2 place Lamartine). Recently there has been talk of building a replica of the house on the site, on the northern edge of the roundabout in the place Lamartine. The building that lay immediately behind the Yellow House remains and is still a café, the Civette de l'Arlésienne. Although the interior has lost its original character, the view of the ramparts from its windows must be similar to Vincent's view from his studio window in the Yellow House.

On the site of part of the 'Poet's Garden', where Vincent often painted, there is still a small sandy area on the Rhône side of the square where old men play *boules* and an even smaller patch of garden. A few paces away by the riverbank is the spot where Vincent painted the Rhône under a starry night, with the Trinquetaille Bridge in the distance. On the opposite side of the square was the district that Vincent called 'the street of the kind girls'. Although a few old houses remain here, most of the area has been replaced by post-war flats and the prostitutes have long since departed.

For those retracing Vincent's footsteps, the most important site in Arles is the hospital where he was treated for his mutilated ear. Dating from 1573, it was closed in 1974 and has now been converted into an arts centre, the Espace Van Gogh. The other popular site for visitors is the drawbridge on the Canal de Bouc, similar to the one that Vincent painted—the Pont de Langlois—which was demolished in 1926.

No visit to Arles is complete without a look at the surrounding countryside: the fields and orchards, bathed in the bright sunlight that attracted Vincent to the Midi. To get a view similar to that in Vincent's 'Road to Tarascon', take the Montmajour turn-off from the Tarascon road, just over a mile north of the place Lamartine.

Montmajour, two miles further on, is where Vincent drew the dramatic ruins of the Benedictine abbey. From here there is a view over the Crau, the fields where Vincent painted his harvest scenes. Three miles beyond Montmajour lies Fontvieille, the village where Vincent visited the Belgian artist, Boch. Nearby is the windmill of Alphonse Daudet.

The Mediterranean fishing village of Saintes-Maries-de-la-Mer, where Vincent painted for five days, is twenty-five miles south of Arles across the mud flats of the Camargue. The drive, with its views of a landscape full of birds and wild horses, is still as charming as it was in Vincent's day. The village, dominated by its church, is a delightful fishing port.

Saint-Rémy

Saint-Rémy, where Vincent retreated to the asylum, is seventeen miles northeast of Arles (by road it can be reached via the dramatic hill town of Les Baux). After the bustle of Arles the small town of Saint-Rémy is a peaceful haven, with a network of narrow streets surrounded by the medieval ramparts. The elegant Estrine mansion, in the centre of the town, is being converted into an arts centre dedicated to Van Gogh.

The asylum of Saint-Paul-de-Mausole, which is half a mile to the south of the town in the avenue Edgar Leroy, is still a mental hospital and its doors are firmly barred to visitors. Vincent's small bedroom, which in his day was like a prison cell, was modernized in the 1960s. Only the view from his window at the back remains relatively unchanged: the garden (then a wheatfield), the wall encircling the asylum and the jagged peaks of the Alpilles. At the front of the asylum, again closed to visitors, is the small grove of trees and the fountain where Vincent painted.

Adjacent to the mental hospital is the Romanesque cloister and church of Saint-Paul-de-Mausole, which are both open to the public. A visit here leaves an impression of the tranquillity of the asylum and gives a good view of the countryside where Vincent

painted. Just five minutes' walk away are the dramatic Graeco-Roman ruins of Glanum. Also nearby are curious quarries, some dating back to Roman days, which Vincent painted as well. All around are olive groves, orchards and twisted cypress trees. In the distance are the distorted forms of the Alpilles. There are marvellous walks in these mountains and a track with dramatic views runs along their crest.

The North: Paris and Auvers

Before Vincent left for Provence, he had lived in Paris for two years. For most of this time he and Theo stayed at 54 rue Lepic, in a second-floor flat overlooking the street, and the building now has a plaque. Rue Lepic starts at the boulevard de Clichy, then the centre of the artists' *quartier*. Among the artists living there when Vincent was in Paris were Degas (6 boulevard de Clichy), Renoir (no. 11), John Russell (no. 73), Cormon (no. 104), Seurat (no. 128 *bis*) and Signac (no. 130).

At the top end of rue Lepic was the village of Montmartre, with its mills and vineyards, as well as a growing number of restaurants and cafés. A visit to the Museum of Montmartre (17 rue St-Vincent) gives a good idea of what the area used to be like. Tradition has it that Vincent's painting of 'La Guinguette' was done at what is now the Auberge de la Bonne Franquette (18 rue St-Rustique).

When Vincent left Saint-Rémy for Auvers he spent four days with Theo and his new wife Jo in their fourth-floor flat at 8 cité Pigalle, off the rue Pigalle. The block of flats still stands, but there is no plaque there.

After his time in Provence Vincent moved to Auvers-sur-Oise, twenty-two miles north of Paris (now accessible by train from the Gare du Nord, via Pontoise). It was already popular among painters and Daubigny, Pissarro and Cézanne worked there. Even today the small town is astonishingly peaceful considering how close it is to the French capital.

Vincent lodged at the café of the Ravoux family, which is just opposite the town hall (place de la Mairie). The house, with the attic room where Vincent died, is being converted into an arts centre in honour of the centenary of the artist's death. His closest friend here was Dr Gachet, and his house still stands (78 rue du Dr Gachet).

The church, which Vincent painted against a deep blue sky, lies in the east of the village. Across the road from the church is the cemetery where Vincent and Theo are both buried, their simple gravestones lying against the wall. Beyond the cemetery and the church are the wheatfields that Vincent painted during his last weeks.

Collections of Van Gogh's work

There are several collections of Vincent's paintings. The finest are both in the Netherlands: the Van Gogh Museum in Amsterdam (7 Paulus Potterstraat) and the Kröller-Müller Museum in Otterlo (set in the De Hoge Veluwe national park near Arnhem). The Musée d'Orsay in Paris (62 rue de Lille) has the best selection of his paintings outside the Netherlands and an extensive collection of pictures by his contemporaries, including Gauguin.

Further Reading

The three-volume *Complete Letters of Vincent van Gogh* (Thames & Hudson, 1958) reproduces virtually all the published letters of the artist. The letters are all numbered and these numbers are given at the end of each extract in this present book. Vincent rarely dated his letters and the dates given in this book have been deduced by scholars. *The Complete Van Gogh* by Jan Hulsker (Phaidon, 1980) illustrates all the paintings and drawings. Among the best general biographies of the artist, although now dated, is *Vincent van Gogh* by Marc Tralbaut (Chartwell Books, 1969).

The catalogues of two exhibitions held at New York's Metropolitan Museum of Art contain a great deal of new research on Van Gogh's period in Provence. These are *Van Gogh in Arles* (Abrams, 1984) and *Van Gogh in Saint-Rémy and Auvers* (Abrams, 1986), both by Ronald Pickvance.

Among works in French the following are recommended. *Van Gogh à Paris* is the catalogue of the exhibition held at the Musée d'Orsay in 1988. *La Provence de Van Gogh* by Jean-Paul Clébert and Pierre Richard (Edisud, 1981) is useful. *Van Gogh et Arles* is the catalogue of the exhibition held in the Espace Van Gogh in Arles in 1989 to mark the centenary of the artist's stay in the town. *Vincent van Gogh à Auvers-sur-Oise* by Alain Mothe (Valhermeil, 1987) is an important study.

Illustration Acknowledgements

Archives of Villeroy & Boch: 15

Archiv für Kunst und Geschichte, Berlin: 27, 42, 46

British Museum, London: 59 (Reproduced by Courtesy of the Trustees)

Cincinnati Art Museum: 155 (Bequest of Mary E. Johnston)

Cleveland Museum of Art, Ohio: 111 (Gift of the Hanna Fund)

Courtauld Institute Galleries, London; 109 (Bridgeman Art Library, London)

Fine Arts Museums of San Francisco: 14 (Memorial Gift from Dr T. Edward and Tullah Hanley, Bradford, Pennsylvania)

Fogg Art Museum, Harvard University: 78 (Bridgeman Art Library, London)

Folkwang Museum, Essen: 99, 129 (Giraudon, Paris), 136

Hermitage Museum, Leningrad: 93 (Bridgeman Art Library, London)

Hulton-Deustch Collection, London: 13

Kunsthaus, Zurich: 37, 146.

Kunstmuseum, Basel: 153 (Giraudon, Paris)

Kunstmuseum, Solothurn: 134 (Swiss Institute for Art Research)

Kunstmuseum, Winterthur: 51 (Bridgeman Art Library, London), 97

Metropolitan Museum of Art, New York: 143 (Gift of Adele R. Levy)

Musée d'Orsay, Paris: 66, 91, 149 (Giraudon, Paris), 133 (Bridgeman Art Library, London), 151 (Scala Instituto Fotografico, Florence)

Museum of Modern Art, New York: 115 (Abby Aldrich Rockefeller Bequest), 124 (Archiv für Kunst und Geschichte, Berlin)

Nasjonalgalleriet, Oslo: 39 (Dimensions 486 × 600)

National Gallery, London: 64, 86 (Reproduced by Courtesy of the Trustees)

National Museum of Wales, Cardiff: 148

Netherlands Institute for Art History, The Hague: 73, 119

Neue Pinakothek, Munich: 65 (Archiv für Kunst und Geschichte, Berlin)

Ny Carlsberg Glyptothek, Copenhagen: 123 (Bridgeman Art Library, London)

Oskar Reinhart Collection, Winterthur: 105 (Archiv für Kunst und Geschichte, Berlin), 110

Philadelphia Museum of Art: 98 (Mrs Rodolphe Meyer de Schauensee), 100 (Bequest of Lisa Norris Elkins (Mrs William M. Elkins)

Private Collections: 47, 75, 101 (Archiv für Kunst und Geschichte, Berlin), 82 (Bridgeman Art Library, London), 47, 79 (Bridgeman Art Library/Christie's, London), 116 (Bridgeman Art Library/Sotheby's, London), 83, 89 (Christie's Colour Library, London), 23 (Edimedia, Paris)

Pushkin Museum, Moscow: 92, 103, 137 (Scala Instituto Fotografico, Florence)

Solomom R Guggenheim Museum, New York: Back Jacket Illustration, 29A/B, 30A/B (Photo: Robert E. Mates © 1990 The Solomon R. Guggenheim Foundation)

State Museum Kröller-Müller, Otterlo: 24, 26, 44, 54, 67 (Bridgeman Art Library), 72, 74, 90, 102, 104, 125, 129 (Lauros-Giraudon), 131 (Edimedia), 145 (Edimedia)

Vincent van Gogh Foundation/National Museum Vincent van Gogh, Amsterdam: Front Jacket Illustration, Half-title Page, Frontispiece, 1, 2, 3, 4, 5, 6, 7, 8, 9, 10, 11, 12, 16, 17, 18, 19, 20, 21, 22, 25, 28, 31, 32 (Roger-Viollet, Paris), 33, 34, 35, 36, 38, 40, 41, 43 (Archiv für Kunst und Geschichte, Berlin), 45, 48, 49, 50, 52, 53, 55, 56, 57, 58, 60, 61, 62, 63, 69, 70, 71, 76, 77, 80, 81, 84, 85, 87, 88, 94, 95, 96, 106, 107, 108, 112, 113, 114, 117, 118, 120, 121, 122, 124, 126, 127, 130, 132, 135, 138, 139, 140, 141, 142, 144, 147, 150, 152, 154, 156, 157, 158, 159 (Archiv für Kunst und Geschichte, Berlin)

Yale University Art Gallery; 68 (Bequest of Stephen Carlton Clark)